Saints

ILLUSTRATED

Saints
ILLUSTRATED

FROM PAUL TO MOTHER TERESA

amber
BOOKS

First published in 2024

Reprinted in 2024, 2025

Copyright © 2024 Amber Books Ltd

Amber Books Ltd
United House
North Road
London N7 9DP
United Kingdom

www.amberbooks.co.uk
Facebook: amberbooks
YouTube: amberbooksltd
Instagram: amberbooksltd
X(Twitter): @amberbooks

ISBN: 978-1-83886-371-5

Editor: Anna Brownbridge
Designer: Mark Batley
Picture Research: Terry Forshaw

Printed and bound in China

TRADITIONAL CHINESE BOOKBINDING
This book has been produced using traditional Chinese bookbinding
techniques, using a method that was developed during the Ming Dynasty
(1368–1644) and remained in use until the adoption of Western binding
techniques in the early 1900s. In traditional Chinese binding, single sheets of
paper are printed on one side only, and each sheet is folded in half, with the
printed pages on the outside. The book block is then sandwiched between two
boards and sewn together through punched holes close to the cut edges of the
folded sheets.

Contents

BEFORE CHRIST

Saints are venerated after their earthly existences because of their holiness, and, naturally, there are a number instrumental to Christ's life. Because they are from the start of the Christian story, places and dates of birth are hazy, and they lived before the canonisation era.

ST RAPHAEL THE ARCHANGEL (3RD–2ND CENTURY BC)

PLACE OF BIRTH: N/A

DATE OF CANONIZATION: N/A

FEAST DAY: 29 SEPTEMBER

PATRONAGE: HEALING

ATTRIBUTES: HOLDING A BOTTLE OR FLASK, WALKING WITH TOBIAS,
SOUNDING A TRUMPET, CARRYING A FISH OR STAFF

St Raphael is an angel who, in the 2nd or 3rd century before Christ's birth, stirred the waters of the Pool of Bethesda, a reservoir in Jerusalem. Jesus later healed a paralyzed man in the waters, and St Raphael is associated with healing. He is prayed to by those seeking his restorative powers but also those looking for good luck on their travels. As told in the Old Testament, St Raphael accompanied Tobit's son Tobias on a journey, during which the angel showed Tobias the healing powers within a fish. As an angel, he neither has a birthplace nor a date of canonization, as he has always been a saint.

ST JOACHIM (75 BC–15 BC)

PLACE OF BIRTH: NAZARETH

DATE OF CANONIZATION: N/A

FEAST DAY: 26 JULY

PATRONAGE: FATHERS, GRANDFATHERS, GRANDPARENTS

ATTRIBUTES: WITH ST ANNE OR ST MARY

Joachim was the father of Mary but he and his wife, Anne, conceived her immaculately. He was a wealthy man who, because of his and Anne's inability to conceive, went out into the desert for 40 days to fast, whereupon angels visited him and promised him and his wife a child. Because of his role in the conception of Mary and Jesus, he is a patron saint of fathers, grandfathers and grandparents, and when he is portrayed visually, it is often with Anne or Mary. In 2021, when Pope Francis announced the World Day for Grandparents and the Elderly, he made it the fourth Sunday in July, close to the feast day of St Joachim.

ST ANNE (BEFORE 49 BC–AFTER AD 4)

PLACE OF BIRTH: BETHLEHEM

DATE OF CANONIZATION: N/A

FEAST DAY: 26 JULY

PATRONAGE: MOTHERS, GRANDMOTHERS,
GRANDPARENTS

ATTRIBUTES: WITH ST JOACHIM OR ST MARY

Anne was the mother of Mary, and, as a saint, she shares her feast day with her husband, Joachim. Similarly, her importance in Jesus's lineage means that she is a patron saint of mothers, grandmothers and grandparents, and is often shown in art with Joachim or Mary. She is thought to have been born around 50 years before the birth of Christ and to have died after it. There has been increasing devotion to St Anne among Catholics since the 12th century, but she is also revered in Islam, and she is mentioned in the Quran as the wife of Imran, which is how Joachim is named in it.

ST MARY THE BLESSED VIRGIN (18 BC–AFTER AD 33)

PLACE OF BIRTH:
HERODIAN KINGDOM OF JUDEA
DATE OF CANONIZATION: N/A
FEAST DAY: 15 AUGUST
PATRONAGE: ALL HUMANITY
ATTRIBUTES: N/A

Being the 'Mother of God', Mary holds a special place among
saints and angels. She is venerated not just for the Immaculate
Conception and being Jesus's mother, but because of her piety
throughout her life and because she herself was immaculately
conceived. However, her later life is rarely mentioned in
the Bible, and there is debate as to the timing and nature of
her death, although she was still alive at Jesus's crucifixion.
Her ascendancy to Heaven – the Assumption of Mary – is
celebrated on 15 August. However, different localities across
the world hold their own Marian festivities throughout the
year, just as various places, groups of people and religious
orders see her as their patron.

ST JOSEPH (1ST CENTURY BC–1ST CENTURY AD)

PLACE OF BIRTH: BETHLEHEM

DATE OF CANONISATION: N/A

FEAST DAY: 19 MARCH

PATRONAGE: A HAPPY DEATH, CARPENTERS

ATTRIBUTES: CARPENTERS' TOOLS, HOLDING BABY JESUS

Joseph was married to the Virgin Mary, the mother of Jesus, and was declared by Pope Pius IX in the 19th century to be both the patron and protector of the Catholic Church. He is the patron saint of a happy death, since he is believed to have died in the presence of Jesus and Mary, as well as of carpenters, since that was his trade. In 1955, Pope Pius XII introduced the feast of St Joseph the Worker on 1 May as an ecclesiastical counterpart to International Workers' Day on the same day. The gospels of both Matthew and Luke trace Joseph's lineage back to King David of Israel.

ST ELIZABETH (1ST CENTURY BC)
PLACE OF BIRTH: N/A
DATE OF CANONIZATION: N/A
FEAST DAY: 5 NOVEMBER
PATRONAGE: PREGNANT WOMEN
ATTRIBUTES: N/A

Elizabeth was the mother of John the Baptist and the maternal aunt of the Virgin Mary. She was childless and older than the typical childbearing age when her husband Zechariah was visited by the Archangel Gabriel, who said that Elizabeth would have a son and he should be named John. According to the Gospel of Luke, John would be 'filled with the Holy Spirit even before he is born'. During her holy pregnancy, Elizabeth spent five months in seclusion and, for three months after, the Virgin Mary visited her, while she, too, was pregnant, with Jesus.

ST GABRIEL THE ARCHANGEL (1ST CENTURY BC)

PLACE OF BIRTH: N/A

DATE OF CANONIZATION: N/A

FEAST DAY: 29 SEPTEMBER

PATRONAGE: COMMUNICATIONS

ATTRIBUTES: TRUMPET

Gabriel has the power to announce God's will and appeared to both Zechariah, the father of John the Baptist, and the Virgin Mary, the mother of Jesus, announcing that each would be having holy sons. Various feast days for Gabriel are recorded: all of them in the spring, which is when the Annunciation took place. However, in 1969, the Vatican amalgamated feast days for angels, meaning that St Gabriel now shares one with both Michael and Raphael on 29 September. As Gabriel heralds and brings forth the word of God, he is the patron saint of people who work in communications and is often pictured with a trumpet.

ANNA THE PROPHETESS (1ST CENTURY BC–1ST CENTURY AD)

PLACE OF BIRTH: N/A

DATE OF CANONISATION: N/A

FEAST DAY: 3 FEBRUARY

PATRONAGE: N/A

ATTRIBUTES: N/A

Anna was an old woman who appeared in the Gospel of Luke prophesizing about Christ's birth. During this time, devout Anna never left the Temple of Jerusalem and would worship there night and day, fasting and praying. She is mentioned as being at the Presentation of Jesus at the Temple, which happened 40 days after his birth, hence Anna's feast day is on 3 February, the day after the Presentation is marked. If Anna is pictured it is normally at the Presentation, with Mary, Joseph and Jesus. According to Luke, Mary and Joseph sacrificed two birds at the ritual, as they could not afford a lamb.

FIRST CENTURY AD

Many of Christ's Disciples – the Apostles – have become saints, as they spread his teachings after the Crucifixion. Martyrdom was common in this period, with Christianity still outlawed, but these saints live on in their patronage, and their attributes in visual depictions of them.

THE HOLY INNOCENTS
(CONTEMPORARIES OF THE INFANT CHRIST)

PLACE OF BIRTH: BETHLEHEM

DATE OF CANONIZATION: N/A

FEAST DAY: 28 DECEMBER

PATRONAGE: BABIES AND FOUNDLINGS

ATTRIBUTES: MARTYRS' PALM, CROWN OF MARTYRDOM

According to the Gospel of Matthew, King Herod ordered the execution of all boys aged two and under in Bethlehem, after he heard that a 'King of the Jews' – Christ – had been born there. Herod had asked the Magi (Three Wise Men) where Christ had been born so that he could worship him, but in a dream, they were warned that Herod wanted to kill the child. As a result, they did not tell Herod, who, furious, ordered the slaughter of the innocent babies. However, by this time Joseph and Mary had taken Jesus to Egypt, having been told by an angel that Herod wanted to kill Jesus. As such, the infants are regarded as the First Martyrs.

ST MARY MAGDALENE
(CONTEMPORARY OF CHRIST)
PLACE OF BIRTH: MAGDALA, ROMAN JUDEA
DATE OF CANONIZATION: N/A
FEAST DAY: 22 JULY
PATRONAGE: PHARMACISTS AND CONVERTS
ATTRIBUTES: ALABASTER BOX OF OINTMENT

Mary Magdalene was present at Jesus's crucifixion, burial and resurrection and is the woman most mentioned in the Gospels outside of Christ's family. In the Gospels, it is written that Jesus exorcized seven demons from her and she became a devoted follower of him, often portrayed in paintings anointing his feet. She also supported Jesus's teachings financially. The portrayal of her as a prostitute began in the 6th century AD. There have also been claims that in her lifetime she travelled as far as France and that she and Jesus produced offspring.

ST PHILIP (1ST CENTURY AD)

PLACE OF BIRTH: BETHSAIDA, GALILEE

DATE OF CANONISATION: N/A

FEAST DAY: 1 MAY

PATRONAGE: BAKERS

ATTRIBUTES: HOLDING A CROSS; WITH LOAVES

One of the 12 Disciples of Jesus, Philip was from Bethsaida, as were Disciples Andrew and Peter. He was present at the Feeding of the 5,000 – when Jesus fed the gathered mass with only five loaves and two fish – and at the Last Supper. There, Philip asked Jesus to show God to the Disciples, and Christ told them about the unity of the Father and Son in him. Philip died in Hierapolis (in modern-day Turkey), and is believed to have preached in that area, as well as in Greece and Syria. He is said to have been crucified upside down after he converted the wife of a Roman proconsul in Hierapolis to Christianity.

ST BARTHOLOMEW (1ST CENTURY AD)

PLACE OF BIRTH: CANA, GALILEE

DATE OF CANONISATION: N/A

FEAST DAY: 24 AUGUST

PATRONAGE: ARMENIAN APOSTOLIC CHURCH

ATTRIBUTES: KNIFE, FLAYED SKIN

Bartholomew was a well-travelled missionary after Jesus's Ascension to Heaven. In many accounts, he is said to have preached as far as India, Ethiopia, Mesopotamia (modern-day Iraq), Parthia (in modern-day Iran) and Armenia. He died in Albanopolis, thought to have been in the Caucasus area, and is said to have been skinned alive after performing several miracles and converting the wife of a king. Many churches take St Batholomew's name, including the Priory Church of St Bartholomew the Great in the City of London, after which the nearby St Bartholomew's (Barts) Hospital is named.

ST MATTHEW (1ST CENTURY AD)

PLACE OF BIRTH: CAPERNAUM, GALILEE

DATE OF CANONISATION: N/A

FEAST DAY: 21 SEPTEMBER

PATRONAGE: TAX COLLECTORS

ATTRIBUTES: ANGEL

Matthew, one of the authors of the Gospels, was one of Jesus's 12 Disciples. In his own Gospel, he recounts that he was a tax collector and was called to follow Jesus while doing his job in Capernaum, the fishing village on the Sea of Galilee where he was born. He is said to have then preached the Gospel in Judea, before travelling further afield and converting Ephigenia of Ethiopia. When he told King Hirtacus that he could not marry Ephigenia because she was now a nun, the king ordered his bodyguard to kill Matthew, making him a martyr. He is often portrayed with an angel, as he and the other three Evangelists – Mark, Luke and John – are attributed with one of the four beings surrounding God's throne in the Book of Revelation.

ST THOMAS (1ST CENTURY AD)
PLACE OF BIRTH: PANSADA, GALILEE
DATE OF CANONISATION: N/A
FEAST DAY: 3 JULY
PATRONAGE: CHRISTIANS IN INDIA
ATTRIBUTES: SPEAR

Known as 'Doubting Thomas' for initially questioning the
resurrection of Jesus when he was told of it, Thomas was
one of the 12 Disciples. When he saw Jesus and his wounds,
he did believe and proclaimed: 'My Lord and my God!' The
Saint Thomas Christians of Kerala, in south India, trace
their origins to Thomas travelling as far as there, preaching
the Gospel. Indeed, there is a shrine on St Thomas' Mount
in Chennai, in the southern Indian state of Tamil Nadu,
where Thomas is believed to have been murdered with a
spear. He is also claimed to have visited China, Indonesia
and even Paraguay.

ST JAMES THE LESS (1ST CENTURY AD)

PLACE OF BIRTH: GALILEE

DATE OF CANONISATION: N/A

FEAST DAY: 3 MAY

PATRONAGE: FULLERS

ATTRIBUTES: FULLER'S CLUB

There were two men named James among the 12 Disciples: one known as James the Less, "Less" meaning younger or shorter, and another called James the Great. James the Less was the brother of the Disciple Matthew, both of whose father was Alphaeus. Some believe that James the Less was the brother of Jesus because James the Less's mother was also called Mary. In Christian art, James the Less is often depicted holding a fuller's club, as he may have been beaten to death with one. As such, one of his patronages is fullers – those who work in cleaning wool.

ST JUDE THADDEUS (1ST CENTURY AD)

PLACE OF BIRTH: GALILEE

DATE OF CANONISATION: N/A

FEAST DAY: 28 OCTOBER

PATRONAGE: DESPERATE OR LOST CAUSES

ATTRIBUTES: AXE

Jude was one of the 12 Disciples and is often also called Thaddeus. He preached widely and was killed in Beirut with an axe. Because many people recounted that praying at Jude's grave resulted in powerful intercessions from the Apostle, St Jude became known as the patron saint of desperate or lost causes. It is also thought that when he would try to help people in the direst of circumstances, to distinguish himself from the similarly named Judas Iscariot, Jesus's betrayer. The Order of Preachers (better known as the Dominicans) embraced the story, and when they took their work to the Americas, they popularized it, hence why St Jude is the unlikely patron saint of the Chicago Police Department.

ST SIMON (1ST CENTURY AD)

PLACE OF BIRTH: CANA, GALILEE

DATE OF CANONISATION: N/A

FEAST DAY: 28 OCTOBER

PATRONAGE: SAWYERS

ATTRIBUTES: BEING SAWN IN TWO

To distinguish him from the Disciple Simon Peter, Simon is often referred to as Simon the Zealot, because of a political party he is thought to have belonged to (the Zealots), or Simon the Canaanite, because of his birthplace. He is often associated with Jude – they share the same feast day – as it is thought that the two preached the Gospel as a team, both being martyred in Beirut in 65AD. However, some believe that he died by being sawn in half in Persia, and others that he reached Roman Britain and was crucified at the settlement of Caistor, in modern-day Lincolnshire.

ST MATTHIAS (1ST CENTURY AD)

PLACE OF BIRTH: JUDEA

DATE OF CANONISATION: N/A

FEAST DAY: 14 MAY

PATRONAGE: ALCOHOLICS

ATTRIBUTES: CROSS

Matthias was chosen by God to replace Judas Iscariot among the Disciples after Judas betrayed Jesus. He is unique among the Disciples because of this, as all the others were chosen by Jesus. Although Matthias was not an original Disciple, Acts of the Apostles states that he had been with Jesus since his baptism by John. He preached in what is now modern-day Turkey and was martyred by being crucified near the Caspian Sea, so he is often portrayed with a cross. He is the patron saint of alcoholics because it is said that he overcame a weakness for drink.

ST JAMES THE GREAT (1ST CENTURY AD)

PLACE OF BIRTH: BETHSAIDA, GALILEE

DATE OF CANONISATION: N/A

FEAST DAY: 25 JULY

PATRONAGE: SPAIN

ATTRIBUTES: PILGRIM'S HAT

James is called 'the Great' to distinguish him from fellow Disciple James the Less, who would have been shorter or younger than him. He was one of the first Disciples to join Jesus and was martyred by Herod Agrippa, grandson of King Herod. His remains are said to have been taken to Santiago de Compostela, in northwestern Spain, the word Santiago being derived from the Latin Sancti Iacobi, meaning St James. Since the early Middle Ages, Santiago de Compostela has been a destination for pilgrims and several routes, known as the Camino de Santiago, have developed to the city.

ST JOHN THE BAPTIST (1ST CENTURY AD)

PLACE OF BIRTH: HERODIAN TETRARCHY
DATE OF CANONISATION: N/A
FEAST DAY: 24 JUNE (BIRTH); 29 AUGUST (MARTYRDOM)
PATRONAGE: VARIOUS
ATTRIBUTES: PLATTER WITH OWN HEAD; POURING WATER FROM HANDS

John was a preacher and a prophet who anticipated a messianic figure greater than himself. He baptized Jesus, from which point Jesus began his ministry. John became a martyr when sentenced to death by Herod Antipas, son of Herod the Great. Apart from the Virgin Mary, he is the only saint who has both his birth and death celebrated each year. As such a major figure, he has widespread patronage. He is the patron saint of the medieval military order the Knights Hospitaller, and many places are named after him – St John's, Newfoundland and Saint John, New Brunswick – as well as the Scottish football club St Johnstone, as he is the patron saint of the city of Perth, where the club is based.

ST VERONICA (1ST CENTURY AD)

PLACE OF BIRTH: JERUSALEM

DATE OF CANONISATION: N/A

FEAST DAY: 12 JULY

PATRONAGE: PHOTOGRAPHERS,

LAUNDRY WORKERS

ATTRIBUTES: CLOTH THAT BEARS THE IMAGE OF CHRIST'S FACE

Moved to sympathy by seeing Jesus carrying his cross to Calvary, Veronica, a local widow, gave him her veil so he could wipe his forehead. When he returned it, the image of his face was captured on it and the resulting relic became known as the Veil of Veronica. The 'Veronica' is one of the Holy Faces of Jesus, a title specific to representations of the face of Jesus. Another example is the Shroud of Turin, which some believe to be the burial cloth of Jesus. It is imprinted with a vision of his face and held in the Chapel of the Holy Shroud in Turin. A piece of fabric in St Peter's Basilica in Rome is believed to be the Veil of Veronica.

ST LUKE THE EVANGELIST (1ST CENTURY AD)

PLACE OF BIRTH: ANTIOCH, SYRIA

DATE OF CANONISATION: N/A

FEAST DAY: 18 OCTOBER

PATRONAGE: PHYSICIANS, SURGEONS, ARTISTS

ATTRIBUTES: A BOOK OR PEN, A BRUSH OR PALETTE,

A PAINTING OF AN ICON OF THE VIRGIN MARY, A WINGED OX OR CALF

A physician from Antioch in Ancient Syria, the author of the Gospel of Luke is believed to have been martyred by being hanged from an olive tree. As Antioch was founded by Greeks and Luke included many references to Greek stories in his writings, it is believed he spoke Greek. He is also believed to be the first icon painter, and he painted pictures of the Virgin Mary and Jesus. A number of early images are ascribed to him, such as the Black Madonna of Częstohowa in Poland. As one of the Evangelists, St Luke is often pictured with one of the four creatures mentioned in Revelation surrounding God's throne, in his case a winged ox or calf.

ST PETER (AD 1–64)

PLACE OF BIRTH: BETHSAIDA, JUDEA

DATE OF CANONISATION: N/A

FEAST DAY: 29 JUNE

PATRONAGE: FISHERMEN; THE PAPACY

ATTRIBUTES: BOOK, PAPAL VESTMENTS

The most prominent Apostle in the New Testament, Peter was the first of the Disciples that the risen Christ appeared to, and he was one of the first leaders of the early Christian Church. However, he started out as a fisherman with his brother and fellow Disciple, Andrew. He is seen as the first bishop of Rome – in effect, the first Pope – and as a saint, he shares his feast day with St Paul, as both were central to the creation of the early Christian Church there. The Vatican's St Peter's Square and St Peter's Basilica are named after him, and like St Paul, he has various patronages since he is such a major figure.

ST PAUL (AD 5–64)

PLACE OF BIRTH: TARSUS, TURKEY

DATE OF CANONISATION: 1867

FEAST DAY: 29 JUNE

PATRONAGE: MALTA; CITY OF LONDON; MISSIONARIES; EVANGELISTS

ATTRIBUTES: BOOK

Paul was a Pharisee who, after Jesus's death, persecuted his early disciples in the Jerusalem area – until Christ appeared to him on the road to Damascus. Paul was then baptized and proclaimed that Jesus was the son of God, before travelling widely as a Christian missionary, including to modern-day Turkey, where he was born. Much of the New Testament is thought to have been written by Paul, and his Letters are often quoted, such as his First Letter to the Corinthians, which is much used at Christian weddings. Paul is the patron saint of Malta, he was shipwrecked there on the way to Rome – where he founded the early Christian Church with the Apostle Peter. He is also the patron saint of the City of London, where St Paul's Cathedral is located, and was formally canonized by Pope Pius IX in 1867.

ST STEPHEN (AD 5–36)

PLACE OF BIRTH: N/A

DATE OF CANONISATION: N/A

FEAST DAY: 26 DECEMBER

PATRONAGE: DEACONS

ATTRIBUTES: MARTYR'S CROWN; MARTYR'S PALM

Stephen is venerated as the first martyr of Christianity. He was a deacon of the early Christian Church in Jerusalem and was accused of blasphemy and stoned to death. Paul – before his conversion – was a participator in Stephen's martyrdom. The 'feast of Stephen' – 26 December – is mentioned in the Christmas carol Good King Wenceslas and the day is a public holiday in many countries. Many churches are named after him, as is the chapel that served as the first debating chamber at the Palace of Westminster, under the reign of Henry III. The French city Saint Etienne also takes its name from him, with Etienne being the French form of Stephen.

ST ANDREW THE APOSTLE (AD 5–60)

PLACE OF BIRTH: BETHSAIDA, GALILEE

DATE OF CANONISATION: N/A

FEAST DAY: 30 NOVEMBER

PATRONAGE: SCOTLAND, ROMANIA, UKRAINE, RUSSIA, FISHERMEN

ATTRIBUTES: A CROSS, A FISHING NET

Jesus called upon Andrew and his brother Peter – who were both fishermen – to be 'fishers of men'. After Jesus's death, Andrew preached as far as Romania, Ukraine and Russia, becoming a patron saint of these countries. He was crucified in Patras, Greece, on what is said to be an X-shaped cross, which has come to be known as a saltire. In the Middle Ages, relics of St Andrew were taken to Scotland, and the saltire – St Andrew's Cross – was adopted as a national symbol, with the town of St Andrews named after him. His feast day is a national holiday in Scotland and in the Catholic Church, and Advent begins on the Sunday nearest his feast day each year.

ST JOHN THE APOSTLE (AD 6–99)

PLACE OF BIRTH: BETHSAIDA, GALILEE

DATE OF CANONISATION: N/A

FEAST DAY: 27 DECEMBER

PATRONAGE: AUTHORS, BOOKSELLERS

ATTRIBUTES: A BOOK, AN EAGLE

The author of the Gospel of John was the youngest of the Apostles and the younger brother of James the Great. He is seen as the 'Beloved Disciple', whom Jesus loved the most. Later, along with Peter, John was central to the foundation of the Church after Jesus's Ascension, and Paul recalled that John, Peter and James the Just were the three 'Pillars of the Church'. In art, John is often portrayed as androgynous, and in Dan Brown's novel The Da Vinci Code, one of the book's characters suggests that the feminine-looking person in Leonardo da Vinci's painting The Last Supper is Mary Magdalene, not John.

ST MARK (AD 12–68)

PLACE OF BIRTH: CYRENE, LIBYA

DATE OF CANONISATION: N/A

FEAST DAY: 25 APRIL

PATRONAGE: VENICE, EGYPT, COPTS

ATTRIBUTES: WINGED LION; WITH A BOOK

After Jesus's Ascension, the author of the Gospel of Mark travelled to Alexandria and founded the Church of Alexandria, and both the Coptic Orthodox and Coptic Catholic churches trace their roots to this event. However, because of his ministry there, pagans in the city tied a rope around his neck and dragged him through the streets until he was dead. St Mark's Square and St Mark's Basilica in Venice are named after him, as is the city's San Marco district, after relics of St Mark were taken from Alexandria to Venice during the 9th century AD.

AD
100 – 400

In this period, Christianity spread across the
Mediterranean and Europe, establishing itself in
Rome. Yet Christians were still persecuted and
subject to gruesome deaths. Common in this
period was women martyred for wanting to devote
themselves to God, and refusing to marry.

STS VICTOR AND CORONA (2ND CENTURY AD)

PLACE OF BIRTH: N/A

DATE OF CANONIZATION: N/A

FEAST DAY: 14 MAY

PATRONAGE: FELTRE, CAUSES INVOLVING MONEY,
SUCH AS GAMBLING OR TREASURE HUNTING

ATTRIBUTES: N/A

Victor was a Christian Roman soldier who was tortured and killed, and Corona was killed for comforting him. Victor's eyes were gouged out and he was beheaded. Corona was bound to two bent palm trees, and was then torn apart when the trunks were released. There is a church named after the pair outside the town of Feltre in northern Italy, which was built by local Crusaders after the First Crusade. The two are patron saints of the town, and Corona – whose name means 'crown' – is invoked as the patron saint of causes involving money. More recently, she has been invoked against the coronavirus pandemic.

ST MICHAEL THE ARCHANGEL (2ND–3RD CENTURY AD)

PLACE OF BIRTH: N/A

DATE OF CANONIZATION: N/A

FEAST DAY: 29 SEPTEMBER

PATRONAGE: POLICE OFFICERS, PARAMEDICS,
THE MILITARY, VATICAN CITY

ATTRIBUTES: SLAYING SATAN, SWORD

St Michael appears in pre-Christian Jewish scriptures as chief of the angels and archangels, and he is also mentioned in Revelation and in the New Testament, in which he does battle with Satan, casting him out of Heaven. He shares a feast day with archangels Raphael and Gabriel, yet it is his name that is given to the celebration Michaelmas. In medieval times, he was seen, with St George, as the patron saint of chivalry, and in the British honours system, the Order of St Michael and St George concerns itself with recognizing chivalry. The Russian city of Arkhangelsk, also known as Archangel, is named after him.

ST APOLLONIA (2ND–3RD CENTURY AD)

PLACE OF BIRTH: ALEXANDRIA, EGYPT

DATE OF CANONIZATION: N/A

FEAST DAY: 9 FEBRUARY

PATRONAGE: DENTISTS

ATTRIBUTES: TONGS, SOMETIMES WITH A TOOTH IN THEM

Apollonia was one of a group of virgin martyrs who were killed in Alexandria during an uprising against Christians. She was tortured and all of her teeth were violently pulled out or shattered, hence why she is a patron saint of dentists. In the Middle Ages, objects that were purported to be her teeth were sold as toothache cures, and in some areas of Italy, St Apollonia is cast in the role of the tooth fairy. There are a number of images of her across English churches, particularly in Devon and East Anglia, and she features in the coat of arms of the British Dental Association.

ST FELICITAS (AD 101–165)

PLACE OF BIRTH: ROME, ITALY

DATE OF CANONIZATION: N/A

FEAST DAY: 23 NOVEMBER

PATRONAGE: PARENTS WHO HAVE LOST A CHILD

ATTRIBUTES: WOMAN WITH SEVEN SONS

Felicitas was the mother of seven martyrs, and she was buried on 23 November, which came to be her feast day. She was a pious Christian woman who converted many to the faith by her example. This aroused the wrath of Roman pagan priests, who lodged a complaint about her with Emperor Marcus Aurelius. He attempted to get her to worship Roman gods, but she and her sons refused. They were all sentenced to death, and she witnessed the deaths of all seven. It is said that she died eight times: once for each of her sons and once for herself.

ST DENIS OF PARIS (3RD CENTURY AD)

PLACE OF BIRTH: ITALY

DATE OF CANONIZATION: N/A

FEAST DAY: 9 OCTOBER

PATRONAGE: FRANCE, PARIS

ATTRIBUTES: CARRYING HIS SEVERED HEAD; A BISHOP'S MITRE

Denis was a bishop of Paris martyred for his faith by decapitation on Montmartre hill. After having his head cut off, he is said to have walked for several miles while holding it and delivering a sermon on repentance. A chapel was raised at the site of his burial by a local Christian woman, Genevieve; it was later expanded into an abbey and basilica, which became the burial place of the kings of France. Around this grew the city of Saint-Denis, now a suburb of Paris. St Denis is one of the 14 Holy Helpers, whose intercession is seen as particularly effective.

ST CHRISTOPHER (3RD CENTURY AD)

PLACE OF BIRTH: CANAAN

DATE OF CANONIZATION: N/A

FEAST DAY: 25 JULY

PATRONAGE: TRAVELLERS, MARINERS, FERRYMEN, ATHLETES

ATTRIBUTES: PORTRAYED AS A GIANT, CARRYING A CHILD

As St Christopher is the patron saint of travellers, figures of him are often worn around the neck, on a bracelet, in a pocket or placed in a vehicle. One story that lends itself to this patronage is that he carried a child across a river and the child revealed himself as Christ. Because of his purported strength, St Christopher is also the patron saint of athletes. The island of Saint Kitts in the Caribbean is named after him and its official name is Saint Christopher Island. Christopher himself was a 3rd-century AD Christian martyr from Canaan who was killed by the Romans.

ST BLAISE (3RD–4TH CENTURY AD)

PLACE OF BIRTH: SEBASTEA, TURKEY

DATE OF CANONIZATION: N/A

FEAST DAY: 3 FEBRUARY

PATRONAGE: WOOL COMBERS, ANIMALS, VETERINARIANS, PHYSICIANS

ATTRIBUTES: ANIMALS, WOOL COMB

One of the 14 Holy Helpers – revered for their level of intercession – Blaise was a physician and bishop of Sebastea, in modern-day Turkey. People flocked to him for his medical skills, and he is also said to have healed animals that came to him on their own for his assistance. He was martyred by the Romans by being beaten, tortured with iron combs and beheaded. He is often portrayed in a cave, surrounded by animals. He is also the patron saint of wool combers due to the similarity between their instruments and the weapon with which he was tortured.

ST CYPRIAN (AD 210–258)
PLACE OF BIRTH: CARTHAGE, TUNISIA
DATE OF CANONIZATION: N/A
FEAST DAY: 16 SEPTEMBER
PATRONAGE: NORTH AFRICA, BERBERS
ATTRIBUTES: N/A

Cyprian was a bishop of Carthage in North Africa who was born into a rich pagan Berber family. He adopted Christianity only after he was baptized aged 35, at which point he gave away a portion of his wealth to the poor of Carthage. He was elected bishop of Carthage but was imprisoned during renewed persecution of Christians by Roman Emperor Valerian, who executed Pope Sixtus II. Cyprian was beheaded while still praying. Cyprian's martyrdom was followed by the martyrdom of eight of his disciples in Carthage.

ST LAWRENCE (AD 225–258)

PLACE OF BIRTH: HUESCA, SPAIN

DATE OF CANONIZATION: N/A

FEAST DAY: 10 AUGUST

PATRONAGE: COMEDIANS, COOKS, CHEFS, HUESCA, FIREFIGHTERS

ATTRIBUTES: HOLDING A GRIDIRON

Lawrence was one of seven deacons of Rome under Pope Sixtus II who were martyred in the persecution of Christians ordered by Roman Emperor Valerian in AD 258. Lawrence had met the future Pope Sixtus II in Zaragoza, and they travelled together from Spain to Rome. The Romans tortured him on a hot gridiron that had burning coals beneath it. Legend has it that after a long time on the gridiron, Lawrence said: 'I'm well done on this side. Turn me over!' From this, St Lawrence derives his patronage of cooks, chefs and comedians.

ST VALENTINE (AD 226–269)

PLACE OF BIRTH: TERNI, ITALY

DATE OF CANONIZATION: N/A

FEAST DAY: 14 FEBRUARY

PATRONAGE: ENGAGED COUPLES, HAPPY MARRIAGES, LOVE

ATTRIBUTES: ROSES, BIRDS

Valentine was a clergyman who ministered to persecuted
Christians in 3rd-century AD Italy and who was martyred on
14 February. One story about Valentine that has contributed
to how he is regarded today as the patron saint of courtly love
is that he performed secret Christian weddings, which then
allowed husbands to avoid conscription into the Roman army.
To remind the men of God's love, Valentine is said to have cut
hearts from parchment to give to them, a possible origin of
the widespread use of hearts on St Valentine's Day.

ST AGATHA (AD 231–251)

PLACE OF BIRTH: CATANIA, SICILY

DATE OF CANONIZATION: N/A

FEAST DAY: 5 FEBRUARY

PATRONAGE: CATANIA, BREAST CANCER PATIENTS, BAKERS,
WET NURSES, RAPE VICTIMS

ATTRIBUTES: PINCERS, BREASTS ON A PLATE

Agatha was a Christian who took a vow of virginity at 15 and
rejected the advances of the Roman prefect Quintianus. To
try to force her to change her mind, he sent her to Aphrodisia,
the keeper of a brothel, and had her imprisoned there. Agatha
was steadfast, however, so he had her tortured, during which
her breasts were torn off with tongs. He intended to have
her burned at the stake, but an earthquake prevented this. St
Peter the Apostle appeared to her and healed her wounds, but
she died in prison. In the Sicilian city of Catania, there is a
major festival in honour of her every February, when Minne
di Sant'Agata – pastries shaped like breasts – are made.

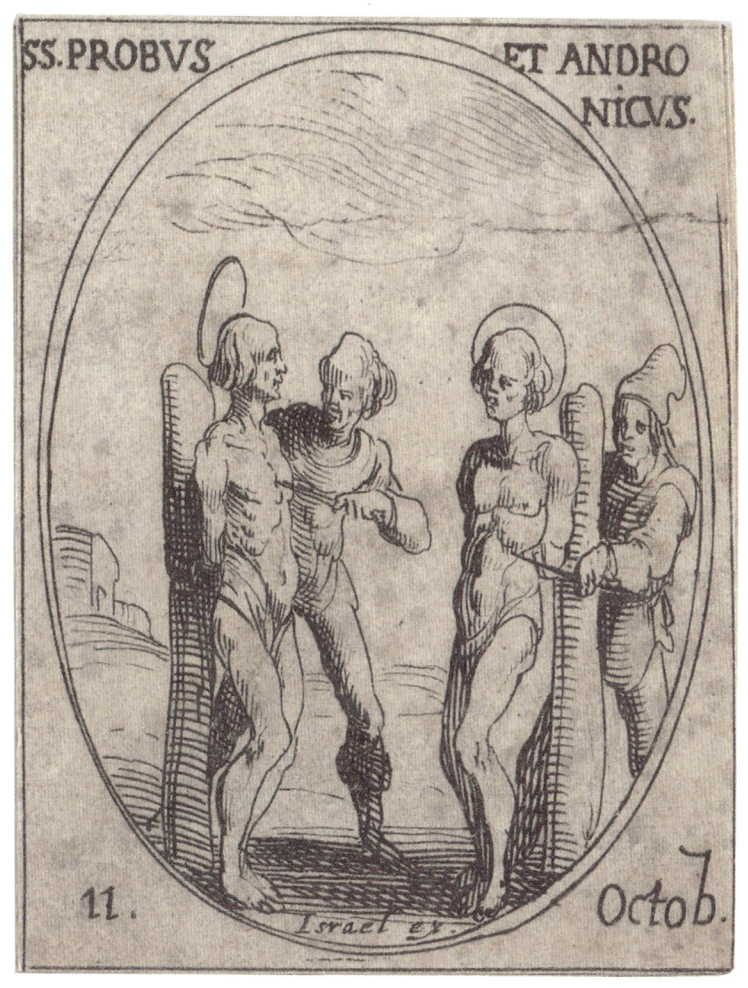

STS ANDRONICUS, PROBUS AND TARACHUS
(c. AD 239–304)

PLACE OF BIRTH: N/A

DATE OF CANONIZATION: N/A

FEAST DAY: 11 OCTOBER

PATRONAGE: N/A

ATTRIBUTES: CROSSES AND SPEARS

This trio of Christian martyrs was tried by Roman governor Numerian Maximus and executed in Tarsus, in modern-day Turkey, as part of the persecution of Christians under Emperor Diocletian. Under torture, Andronicus and Probus (pictured) were cut with knives, and Tarachus was beaten with stones. Andronicus was a member of a prominent family, Probus was a plebeian and Tarachus had been a Roman soldier. They were condemned to death by wild beasts, but the animals would not touch them in the amphitheatre, so they were stabbed instead.

18. Aug.　　　　　3. Maij　　　　　M.u Snyl.fe

S. HELENA, mater Conſtantini Magni Imperatoris, Crucem Dominicam, ſub terra latentem, in monte Golgotha, inuenit ac detexit, anno Chriſti 326.

ST HELENA (c. AD 248–330)
PLACE OF BIRTH: BITHYNIA, TURKEY
DATE OF CANONIZATION: N/A
FEAST DAY: 18 AUGUST
PATRONAGE: ARCHAEOLOGISTS, CONVERTS, NEW DISCOVERIES, SAINT HELENA ISLAND
ATTRIBUTES: CROWN, CROSS, NAILS

Helena was the mother of Constantine the Great, the first Christian Roman emperor. She was born in Bithynia, in modern-day Turkey, which was renamed Helenopolis in her honour. She had Constantine with his father Constantius before Constantius became emperor. On Constantius's death, Constantine became emperor. He stopped the persecution of Christians, and Helena developed a strong interest in the Holy Land. She later visited there and discovered the True Cross. Saint Helena Island in the South Atlantic is named after her.

ST SEBASTIAN (AD 255–288)
PLACE OF BIRTH: NARBONNE, FRANCE
DATE OF CANONIZATION: N/A
FEAST DAY: 20 JANUARY
PATRONAGE: ARCHERS, SOLDIERS
ATTRIBUTES: TIED TO A POST, PILLAR OR TREE;
SHOT BY ARROWS

Although a Christian, Sebastian joined the Roman army, doing so to help the persecuted. Due to his courage, he became one of the captains of the Praetorian Guards. However, his faith was discovered, and he was led to a field so he could be shot. He was tied to a tree and shot with arrows, although these did not kill him. He was rescued and healed by St Irene of Rome, but later was beaten to death with cudgels by the Romans and left in a sewer. In medieval times, he was regarded as a saint with a special ability to protect from plague. The city of San Sebastian in Spain is named after him.

ST NICHOLAS (AD 270–343)

PLACE OF BIRTH: PATARA, TURKEY

DATE OF CANONIZATION: N/A

FEAST DAY: 6 DECEMBER

PATRONAGE: CHILDREN, SAILORS, FISHERMEN

ATTRIBUTES: DRESSED AS A BISHOP, WITH JESUS CHRIST OVER ONE SHOULDER, HOLDING THREE GOLDEN BALLS OR COINS

Nicholas's habit of gift-giving led to the legendary figure of Santa Claus. He is said to have rescued three girls from being forced into prostitution by dropping a sack of gold coins through the window of their house each night for three nights so their father could pay a dowry for each of them. Another story is that he chopped down a tree possessed by a demon and calmed a storm at sea. Due to the many miracles attributed to his intercession, he is known as Nicholas the Wonderworker. He was bishop of Myra, in modern-day Turkey.

ST GEORGE (AD c.270–303)

PLACE OF BIRTH: CAPPADOCIA, TURKEY

DATE OF CANONIZATION: AD 494

FEAST DAY: 23 APRIL

PATRONAGE: ENGLAND, GEORGIA, SOLDIERS

ATTRIBUTES: CLOTHED AS A CRUSADER, SLAYING A DRAGON,
WITH A ST GEORGE'S CROSS

George was a soldier in the Roman army and became a
member of the Praetorian Guard for Emperor Diocletian, but
he was sentenced to death for refusing to recant his Christian
faith. He was decapitated on 23 April in AD 303. George is
said to have slain a dragon that was extorting villagers, and
this story was well-liked by knights of the First Crusade, who
felt that St George was fighting alongside them. Canonized
by Pope Gelasius I, he is especially venerated as a military
saint. As one of the 14 Holy Helpers, St George's patronage
is wide and varied.

ST ANASTASIA (AD 281–300)

PLACE OF BIRTH: ROME, ITALY

DATE OF CANONIZATION: N/A

FEAST DAY: 25 DECEMBER

PATRONAGE: MARTYRS

ATTRIBUTES: MARTYR'S CROSS, BOWL OF MEDICINE

Anastasia was killed during Roman Emperor Diocletian's persecutions against Christians, dying in Sirmium, in modern-day Serbia. She is venerated as a healer and exorcist, and her relics lie in the Cathedral of St Anastasia in Zadar, Croatia. Prior to liturgical reforms in the 12th century, Anastasia had the distinction – unique in the Roman liturgy – of having a special commemoration in the second mass on Christmas Day, the day she died, which is her feast day. She is one of seven women, along with the Virgin Mary, commemorated by name in the Roman Canon of the Mass.

ST LUCY (AD 283–304)

PLACE OF BIRTH: SYRACUSE, SICILY

DATE OF CANONIZATION: N/A

FEAST DAY: 13 DECEMBER

PATRONAGE: THE BLIND

ATTRIBUTES: EYES ON A DISH, WOMAN HITCHED TO A YOKE OF OXEN

Lucy was a Christian martyr whose eyes were gouged out prior to her execution, and St Lucy is often portrayed holding her eyes on a golden plate. From a rich family, she had consecrated her virginity to God so she could give her dowry to the poor. However, her mother, worried about her future, arranged for her to marry a young man from a wealthy pagan family. When the Romans found out about giving away the riches, they tried to seize her but could not do so even when they hitched her to a team of oxen. Similarly, heaps of wood were bundled around her but would not burn. Finally, she was stabbed with a sword.

ST DEVOTA (AD 283–303)

PLACE OF BIRTH: MARIANA, CORSICA

DATE OF CANONIZATION: N/A

FEAST DAY: 27 JANUARY

PATRONAGE: CORSICA, MONACO, MARIANA, MARINERS

ATTRIBUTES: DOVE, BOAT, COAT OF ARMS OF THE PRINCIPALITY OF MONACO

Devota is the patron saint of Corsica and Monaco. She was
killed by Roman forces after she refused to perform a sacrifice.
Her body was dragged through rocks and brambles prior to her
execution. After her death, the Roman governor ordered that
her body be burned so it could not be venerated. However,
her body was saved from the flames by Christians and put on
a boat for Africa. The boat was blown off course until a dove
guided it to Les Gaumates, part of the Principality of Monaco.
There, a chapel was built in her honour, and it still stands today.

ST CATHERINE OF ALEXANDRIA (AD 287–305)

PLACE OF BIRTH: ALEXANDRIA, EGYPT

DATE OF CANONIZATION: N/A

FEAST DAY: 25 NOVEMBER

PATRONAGE: TEACHERS, GIRLS, LAWYERS, LIBRARIANS

ATTRIBUTES: BREAKING WHEEL, SWORD, DOVE, BRIDAL VEIL, BOOK

A noted scholar, St Catherine was martyred at the hands of the Roman Emperor Maxentius. She had rebuked him for persecuting Christians, and after he imprisoned her, a dove from Heaven fed her. Maxentius then tried to win her over by proposing marriage, but she refused. Execution was attempted by forcing a spiked breaking wheel over her, but when she touched it, it shattered. She was then beheaded. Such wheels have since become known as Catherine wheels, and a circular firework has been named after them.

ST AGNES (AD 291–304)

PLACE OF BIRTH: ROME, ITALY

DATE OF CANONIZATION: N/A

FEAST DAY: 21 JANUARY

PATRONAGE: GIRLS, CHASTITY, VIRGINS, VICTIMS OF SEXUAL ABUSE

ATTRIBUTES: A LAMB

From a wealthy family, Agnes attracted many suitors. After taking an oath of religious purity, she was dragged naked through the streets to a brothel. However, the men who tried to rape her were struck blind. When she was tied to a stake, the wood would not burn, so she was beheaded. She is often painted with a lamb, to signify her innocence and purity. Constantina, the daughter of the first Christian Roman Emperor Constantine I, is said to have been cured of leprosy after praying at Agnes's tomb.

ST PHILOMENA (AD 291–304)
PLACE OF BIRTH: CORFU, GREECE
DATE OF CANONIZATION: 1837
FEAST DAY: 11 AUGUST
PATRONAGE: INFANTS, BABIES, YOUTH
ATTRIBUTES: ANCHOR, ARROWS

Philomena was a virgin martyr who became the patron saint of infants, babies and youth. She had taken a vow of virginity for Christ's sake and refused to be the wife of the Roman Emperor Diocletian, for which he unleashed upon her a series of torments: scourging; an attempt at drowning with an anchor attached to her; and being shot with arrows. It is said that two angels cut the anchor rope and returned her to the riverbank and that some of the arrows fired at her turned back and killed six of the archers, with the remainder becoming Christians. She was eventually decapitated. She was officially canonized by Pope Gregory XVI.

ST FORTUNATUS OF SPOLETO (4TH CENTURY AD)

PLACE OF BIRTH: MONTEFALCO, ITALY
DATE OF CANONISATION: N/A
FEAST DAY: 1 JUNE
PATRONAGE: MONTEFALCO
ATTRIBUTES: ROD BURSTING INTO LEAF

Fortunatus, a parish priest near the ancient city of Spoleto, in Italy, became noted after his death for his charity and love for the poor. One day, when he was ploughing a field, he found two coins of apparently little value and put them in his pocket. That evening, upon meeting a poor man on the road, Fortunatus decided to give them to him, at which point sunlight illuminated the two coins, making them shine like gold. So as not to be tempted by avarice, he handed the treasures to the man and quickly hurried away. He is the patron saint of the hilltop town where he was born: Montefalco. When he died, the rod that he used to drive his oxen was staked into the ground and burst into leaf.

ST JULIAN THE HOSPITALLER (4TH CENTURY AD)

PLACE OF BIRTH: LE MANS, FRANCE

DATE OF CANONIZATION: N/A

FEAST DAY: 12 FEBRUARY

PATRONAGE: BOATMEN, FERRYMEN, HOTEL-KEEPERS, PILGRIMS, TRAVELLERS

ATTRIBUTES: CARRYING A LEPER THROUGH A RIVER, HOLDING AN OAR

After killing his parents by accident, Julian devoted the rest of his life to helping others. He made a pilgrimage to Rome with his wife. Near a river, they built a hospice to welcome weary and sick travellers. Julian also helped them across the river. The murder of his parents was the culmination of a curse that his father had witnessed witches put on Julian the night of his birth. Devotion to St Julian started in the Maltese islands in the 15th century after discovery of his relics in the city of Macerata, although a stained-glass depiction of him in Chartres Cathedral in France dates to the 13th century.

ST MARTIN OF TOURS (4TH CENTURY AD)

PLACE OF BIRTH: SAVARIA, HUNGARY

DATE OF CANONIZATION: N/A

FEAST DAY: 11 NOVEMBER

PATRONAGE: FRENCH THIRD REPUBLIC, HORSES, RIDERS

ATTRIBUTES: MAN ON HORSEBACK

Martin of Tours, also known as Martin the Merciful, was the patron saint of the Third French Republic. He converted to Christianity when young and joined the Roman cavalry, serving in France. However, he left the military to become a disciple of Hilary of Poitiers, ultimately becoming the bishop of Tours. His shrine in Tours is a stopping point for pilgrims on the way to Santiago de Compostela, and his cult was revived during the Franco-Prussian War of the 1870s. St Martin-in-the-Fields church in central London is named after him, as was Martin Luther.

ST BASIL THE GREAT (AD 330–378/9)

PLACE OF BIRTH: PONTUS POLEMONIACUS, TURKEY

DATE OF CANONIZATION: N/A

FEAST DAY: 2 JANUARY

PATRONAGE: CAPPADOCIA, MONKS, EDUCATION

ATTRIBUTES: HOLDING A GOSPEL BOOK OR SCROLL

Basil was the bishop of Caesarea Mazaca in Cappadocia, Turkey. Apart from his work as a theologian, he was known for his care for the poor and underprivileged. He established guidelines for monastic life, focusing on community, liturgical prayer and manual labour, and he is known for his asceticism (depriving himself of sensual pleasures). His parents were known for their Christian piety, and his maternal grandfather was a Christian martyr, executed in the years before Constantine I's conversion.

ST MONICA (AD 332–387)

PLACE OF BIRTH: THAGASTE, ALGERIA
DATE OF CANONIZATION: N/A
FEAST DAY: 27 AUGUST
PATRONAGE: MARRIED WOMEN, DIFFICULT MARRIAGES,
DISAPPOINTING CHILDREN, VICTIMS OF ADULTERY, SANTA MONICA
ATTRIBUTES: N/A

The mother of Augustine of Hippo, Monica is a North African saint. She endured her husband's adultery and her son's wayward early life, remaining devout. Augustine wrote about her pious acts in his *Confessions*, and she is said to have wept every night for him. At this time, she was visited by a bishop, who said: 'The child of those years shall never perish.' She followed Augustine to Rome and Milan, where she witnessed him convert to Christianity after 17 years of resistance. The city of Santa Monica in California is named after Monica.

ST AMBROSE (AD 339–397)

PLACE OF BIRTH: TRIER, GERMANY

DATE OF CANONIZATION: N/A

FEAST DAY: 7 DECEMBER

PATRONAGE: MILAN,

BEEKEEPERS

ATTRIBUTES: BEEHIVES

When he was an infant, a swarm of bees settled on Ambrose's face and left behind a drop of honey, which his father is said to have considered a sign of the boy's honeyed tongue and future eloquence. From a Roman family, Ambrose would go on to become the Roman governor of Aemilia-Liguria in Milan. From this position, he was made bishop of Milan. Ambrose led an austere life and often gave to the poor. He has been credited with composing the 'Te Deum' hymn, and he also had a notable influence on Augustine of Hippo, whom he helped convert to Christianity.

ST AUGUSTINE OF HIPPO (AD 354–430)

PLACE OF BIRTH: THAGASTE, ALGERIA

DATE OF CANONIZATION: 1303

FEAST DAY: 28 AUGUST

PATRONAGE: THEOLOGIANS, PHILOSOPHERS

ATTRIBUTES: MITRE, BOOK

Augustine was a theologian, philosopher and the bishop of Hippo Regis in Roman North Africa. He helped formulate the doctrine of original sin and made significant contributions to the development of 'just war' theory. Already widely seen as a saint, he was recognized as a Doctor of the Church by Pope Boniface VIII in 1303. Of Berber origin, Augustine's mother was a Christian and his father converted to Christianity on his deathbed. However, he did not initially adopt the faith, only doing so at the age of 31, when he read the writings of St Paul.

ST PATRICK (AD c.386–c.461)

PLACE OF BIRTH: BRITAIN

DATE OF CANONISATION: N/A

FEAST DAY: 17 MARCH

PATRONAGE: IRELAND

ATTRIBUTES: HOLDING A SHAMROCK, REPELLING SERPENTS

St Patrick is credited with having brought Christianity to
Ireland, but, like many early saints, he was never officially
canonized, having lived before the current rules of the Catholic
Church regarding canonization. Nevertheless, he is seen as the
patron saint of Ireland, and the Irish and people of Irish descent
around the world widely celebrate his feast day. He was born
in Britain and taken as a slave by Irish pirates to Ireland, where
he stayed for six years. Feeling that God had helped him return
to Britain, he went back to Ireland as a Christian missionary to
spread the word. He used the three-leaved shamrock plant to
show how three people exist in God: the Father, Son and Holy
Spirit. He is also said to have banished snakes from Ireland.

L. de la Hire Inue

AD
400 – 1000

With the Roman Empire adopting Christianity, martyrdom waned and the Vatican became the centre of the Christian church. Christianity spread into the outer reaches of Europe, and it became firmly established in political systems, with leaders becoming saints.

ST ALEXIUS OF ROME (4TH–5TH CENTURY AD)

PLACE OF BIRTH: ROME, ITALY

DATE OF CANONISATION: N/A

FEAST DAY: 17 JULY

PATRONAGE: BEGGARS

ATTRIBUTES: MAN LYING BENEATH A STAIRCASE

Alexis was a Greek monk who lived in anonymity. In one version of his story, he lived as a beggar and gave the alms he received to other poor people. In another, he fled his arranged marriage to serve God. Thereafter, he lived an ascetic life, many years of which were spent living under a staircase. He was venerated in the Eastern Church before he was revered in the West. In 972, Pope Benedict VII added Alexis's name to a church in Rome dedicated to St Boniface and its associated monastery. Many of Alexis's relics are found in churches around Greece.

ST LEO THE GREAT (AD 400–461)

PLACE OF BIRTH: TUSCANY, ITALY

DATE OF CANONISATION: N/A

FEAST DAY: 10 NOVEMBER

PATRONAGE: POPES

ATTRIBUTES: PAPAL VESTMENTS, STAFF

Pope Leo I, from an aristocratic Roman family, was bishop of Rome and the first pope to be called 'the Great'. In 452 AD, he met Attila the Hun and persuaded him to refrain from invading Italy. Paul the Deacon, in the 8th century AD, related that an enormous man dressed in priestly robes and armed with a sword, visible only to Attila, threatened Attila and his army with death during his conversation with Leo. It was during Leo's papacy that the term 'Pope', which had previously meant any bishop, came to exclusively mean the bishop of Rome.

ST GENEVIEVE (AD c.419–c.500)

PLACE OF BIRTH: NANTERRE, FRANCE

DATE OF CANONISATION: N/A

FEAST DAY: 3 JANUARY

PATRONAGE: PARIS

ATTRIBUTES: BREAD, KEYS

St Genevieve is the patron saint of Paris and moved there from her birthplace of Nanterre and dedicated herself to Christian life. She is said to have saved Paris by leading a 'prayer marathon' that diverted Attila the Hun's troops away from the city. And in 464, when the Germanic king Childeric I was besieging the city, she acted as an intermediary between the city and its invaders, collecting food and convincing Childeric to release prisoners. It was Genevieve who erected the chapel to Denis, who was to become the patron saint of France.

ST BRIGID OF IRELAND (AD c.451–c.525)

PLACE OF BIRTH: FAUGHART, IRELAND

DATE OF CANONISATION: N/A

FEAST DAY: 1 FEBRUARY

PATRONAGE: IRELAND, KILDARE, BLACKSMITHS

ATTRIBUTES: BRIGID'S CROSS

St Brigid is the 'mother saint' of Ireland, and from 2023 her feast day, 1 February, has been celebrated with a public holiday. She was an abbess who founded Kildare Abbey and several other convents there. She performed a number of miracles, even from when she was a child, and often gave to the poor. She is also credited with founding a school of art, which included metalwork. 'Kilbride' means 'Church of Brigid', and there are many places called that in Ireland, as well as in Scotland. St Bride's Church, in London's Fleet Street (and known as the 'journalists' church') is named after her. A simple cross made out of straw or reeds is also named after her.

ST BENEDICT (AD 480–547)

PLACE OF BIRTH: NURSIA, ITALY

DATE OF CANONISATION: 1220

FEAST DAY: 11 JULY

PATRONAGE: EUROPE

ATTRIBUTES: BELL, MAN IN BENEDICTINE COWL

Benedict was an Italian monk who wrote a set of rules for monks to follow. Known as the Rule of Saint Benedict, this was widely adopted by religious communities founded in the Middle Ages, and the Order of Saint Benedict – often known as the Black Monks because of the colour of their robes – is based on it. As such, he is regarded by some as the founder of Western Christian monasticism. He also founded a number of communities for monks. He was officially canonized by Pope Honorius III in 1220 and was named patron protector of Europe in 1964 by Pope Paul VI.

Sv. Skola stika.

ST SCHOLASTICA (c.480–543)

PLACE OF BIRTH: NURSIA, ITALY

DATE OF CANONISATION: N/A

FEAST DAY: 10 FEBRUARY

PATRONAGE: BENEDICTINE NUNS

ATTRIBUTES: IN BENEDICTINE RELIGIOUS HABIT

Born to wealthy parents, Scholastica was the twin sister of St Benedict and is regarded as the founder of the Benedictine nuns. She was dedicated to God from an early age and established a hermitage near Monte Cassino, which became the first convent of Benedictine nuns. She would often visit her brother and they would discuss sacred texts and issues. She died while she was staying with Benedict, and three days later, he saw her soul rising to Heaven in the form of a shining white dove. It is said that she foretold her death.

ST GOBNAIT (6TH CENTURY AD)

PLACE OF BIRTH: COUNTY CLARE, IRELAND
DATE OF CANONISATION: N/A
FEAST DAY: 11 FEBRUARY
PATRONAGE: BEES
ATTRIBUTES: BEES, BEEHIVES, DEER

Gobnait established a convent after fleeing a family feud and being visited by an angel on Inisheer in the Aran Islands. The angel told her to look for a place where nine white deer were grazing. She found the deer at what is now called St Gobnet's Wood in County Cork, where she founded her nunnery. She kept bees and is said to have driven off a thief trying to steal cattle by sending a swarm after him. On Inisheer, there are the remains of a church called St Gobnet's, where there is said to be evidence of an old beehive hut and that the site had been in use since the 6th century.

STA FLORENTINA

ST FLORENTINA OF CARTAGENA (6TH–7TH CENTURY AD)

PLACE OF BIRTH: CARTAGENA, SPAIN

DATE OF CANONISATION: N/A

FEAST DAY: 20 JUNE

PATRONAGE: PLASENCIA

ATTRIBUTES: BOOK

Florentina was the sister of three bishops, and one of them, Leander, would become the Archbishop of Seville. The siblings had lost their parents at a young age, and Florentina was placed under the guardianship of Leander, who had taken monastic vows. He encouraged her to embrace an ascetic life without worldly pleasures, and Leander wrote a book spelling out how she – and the nuns at the community she established – should live. The community was near Ecija, in Andalusia, and St Florentina lives on as the patron saint of the city of Plasencia, north of there in Extremadura.

ST COLUMBA (AD 521–597)

PLACE OF BIRTH: GARTAN, IRELAND
DATE OF CANONISATION: N/A
FEAST DAY: 9 JUNE
PATRONAGE: DERRY, IRELAND, SCOTLAND
ATTRIBUTES: MONK'S ROBES

Columba was an Irish abbot credited with spreading Christianity in Scotland, having founded an abbey on the island of Iona. Born in the north of Ireland, he sailed to the west coast of Scotland with 12 companions, and among the stories of miracles he performed in trying to convert the locals was one in which he arguably defeated the Loch Ness Monster. He was said to have banished a ferocious 'water beast' to the depths of the River Ness. Along with St Patrick and St Brigid, he is considered one of the three patron saints of Ireland.

POPE ST GREGORY THE GREAT (AD 540–604)

PLACE OF BIRTH: ROME, ITALY
DATE OF CANONISATION: N/A
FEAST DAY: 3 SEPTEMBER
PATRONAGE: STUDENTS, TEACHERS
ATTRIBUTES: DOVE

The bishop of Rome from 590 AD until his death, Gregory initiated the first large-scale mission from Rome, the Gregorian mission, to convert Anglo-Saxons to Christianity. A Roman senator's son, he lived in a monastery he established on his family's estate before becoming papal ambassador and then pope. He was the first pope from a monastic background. He is a Doctor of the Church and one of the Latin Fathers, who created the intellectual and doctrinal basis of the Church. Protestant reformer John Calvin admired Gregory greatly and said he was the last good pope. Gregory is often portrayed with a dove, which was said to be present when he was dictating his homilies on Ezekiel to his secretary.

ST HUNNA (7TH CENTURY AD)

PLACE OF BIRTH: ALSACE, FRANCE

DATE OF CANONISATION: 1520

FEAST DAY: 15 APRIL

PATRONAGE: LAUNDRESSES

ATTRIBUTES: WASHING BASKET

Hunna was the daughter of a duke and duchess who married a nobleman called Huno of Hunnaweyer. Her family was influenced by former bishop and hermit St Daedalus of Nevers to help the poor. While her husband was away for diplomatic and political reasons, Hunna would visit her neighbours and care for the sick, cooking and cleaning for them as well as washing their clothes. This earned her the name of 'Holy Washerwoman'. She would also look after children. Her son was named after Daedalus and became a monk.

S. ALENA Virgo et Martyr
17. Iunij.

ST ALENA (AD 601–640)

PLACE OF BIRTH: DILBEEK, BELGIUM

DATE OF CANONISATION: 1193

FEAST DAY: 24 JUNE

PATRONAGE: EYE PROBLEMS

ATTRIBUTES: A PRINCESS WITH AN ARM TORN OFF

Alena was born to pagan parents and was baptized without their knowledge. She attended mass secretly. Trying to resist being forced home by her father, she lost an arm and died of her injuries. The arm was taken by an angel to the chapel where she worshipped. When Alena's parents saw this, they converted to Christianity. It is also claimed that a duke had his eyesight restored after praying at her grave. Her feast day is recognised as 24 June in the English-speaking world and on various dates in June and December elsewhere.

ST GERTRUDE OF NIVELLES (AD c.628–659)

PLACE OF BIRTH: LANDEN, BELGIUM

DATE OF CANONISATION: 1677

FEAST DAY: 17 MARCH

PATRONAGE: NIVELLES

ATTRIBUTES: RATS, MICE, CATS

Gertrude's father, Pippin the Elder, tried to arrange for her to marry a king when she was 10, but she refused and pledged herself to God. Because of the wealth of her family, Gertrude was still besieged by suitors, even when her mother shaved the top of her head, like a monk, to mark out that she was dedicated to religious service. Only her mother's founding of the Abbey of Nivelles, which Gertrude later took over, stopped them. It is reported that Gertrude's good work – her endless charity, fasting and prayer – took a toll on her body and caused her to die early. St Gertrude's association with cats, and how they control populations of plague-carrying rodents, dates from the Black Death of the 15th century, and she was invoked to protect people from it.

ST VIRGIL OF SALZBURG (AD c.700–784)

PLACE OF BIRTH: IRELAND

DATE OF CANONISATION: 1233

FEAST DAY: 27 NOVEMBER

PATRONAGE: SALZBURG

ATTRIBUTES: VESSEL OF SALT

Virgil left his homeland of Ireland intending to visit the Holy Land but settled in France. In Ireland, he had been abbot of Aghaboe and bishop of Ossory, where he was known as the 'Geometer' because of his knowledge of geography – he was an early believer that the Earth is a sphere. He became an adviser to the Frankish king Pippin the Younger, and after spending two years in Cressy, he went to Bavaria, where he founded the monastery of Chiemsee. He was then made abbot of St Peter's Abbey in Salzburg, where he was later bishop. From there, he converted Alpine Slavs to Christianity and sent missionaries to Hungary. He is often portrayed carrying a vessel of salt, given that the 'salz' in Salzburg means 'salt'.

ST WILLIBALD (AD c.700–c.787)

PLACE OF BIRTH: WESSEX, ENGLAND

DATE OF CANONISATION: 938

FEAST DAY: 7 JULY

PATRONAGE: EICHSTATT

ATTRIBUTES: BOOK

Willibald was reportedly the first Englishman to visit the Holy Land. His father, Richard the Pilgrim, a chieftain of Wessex, had embarked on a journey there with Willibald but died en route, and was buried in Lucca, Italy. On his return from the Holy Land, Willibald stayed at the Benedictine community in Monte Cassino, and ended his days in Germany, doing missionary work in Eichstatt. At the age of three, Willibald had suffered a violent illness, and his parents vowed to commit Willibald to a monastic life if God spared him. So, at age five, he had entered the Benedictine monastery at Waldheim, now Bishop's Waltham, in Hampshire, where he learned the ways of 'pious rootlessness'.

ST CHRODEGANG (AD c.712–766)

PLACE OF BIRTH: HESBAYE, BELGIUM
DATE OF CANONISATION: N/A
FEAST DAY: 6 MARCH
PATRONAGE: METZ
ATTRIBUTES: BOOK, MITRE

Chrodegang was bishop of the French city of Metz when it was under Frankish rule and founded and helped a number of abbeys. He wrote the 'Rule of Chrodegang' for them, consisting of 34 chapters and based on the Rule of Benedict. However, his focus was on community work rather than on monastic life. The 'Rule of Chrodegang' found its way to Ireland, and there are nine places in Ireland where communities stemming from it were established. He was chancellor and prime minister to Frankish political and military leader Charles Martel.

ST PAULINUS II OF AQUILEIA (AD c.726–802/804)

PLACE OF BIRTH: PREMARIACCO, ITALY

DATE OF CANONISATION: 938

FEAST DAY: 11 JANUARY

PATRONAGE: N/A

ATTRIBUTES: BOOK

Paulinus arranged for the peaceful Christianization of Europe's nomadic Avars as well as the Alpine Slavs. For this, he is known as the apostle of the Slovenes. He was ordained into the priesthood after going to school in Cividale, in northern Italy, and then became a teacher himself. When the King of the Franks, Charlemagne, had just conquered all of Lombard (in northern Italy), he made Paulinus royal 'master of grammar'. Paulinus was then appointed Patriarch of Aquileia, the ancient city at the northern end of the Adriatic, from where he held influence over churches in what is now Slovenia and Croatia.

ST THEOPHANES THE CONFESSOR (AD 758/60–817)

PLACE OF BIRTH: CONSTANTINOPLE, TURKEY

DATE OF CANONISATION: N/A

FEAST DAY: 12 MARCH

PATRONAGE: N/A

ATTRIBUTES: SCROLL

Theophanes was a member of the Byzantine aristocracy who became a monk. His father died when he was three, and Byzantine Emperor Constantine V saw to his education and upbringing at the imperial court. He married at 18 but convinced his wife to lead a life of virginity. In 779 AD, after the death of his father-in-law, they separated by mutual consent to embrace religious life. He entered a monastery and then founded his own. He was present at the Church's Second Council of Nicaea in 787 AD and signed its decrees in defence of the veneration of icons. But when Leo V the Armenian took the Byzantine throne and waged war on the worship of icons, Theophanes was thrown into prison, where he lived only 17 days.

ST ANSGAR (AD 801–865)

PLACE OF BIRTH: CORBIE, FRANCE

DATE OF CANONISATION: 865 AD

FEAST DAY: 3 FEBRUARY

PATRONAGE: SCANDINAVIA

ATTRIBUTES: DRESSED IN ARCHBISHOP'S ATTIRE WITH A MODEL OF A CHURCH

Ansgar was the Archbishop of Hamburg-Bremen and became known as the 'Apostle of the North' because of his travels. He had previously travelled as a missionary to Jutland, part of modern-day Denmark, and then to Sweden. He also helped found the abbey of Corvey, in present-day Germany. He was declared a saint by Pope Nicholas I shortly after his death, and, as the first missionary in the Nordic countries, was later decreed the 'Patron of Scandinavia'. He was born the son of a noble Frankish family. After he had entered religious service, he wore a hair shirt and lived on only bread and water.

ST CYRIL AND ST METHODIUS
(AD 826/7–869 AND AD 815–885)
PLACE OF BIRTH: THESSALONIKA, GREECE
DATE OF CANONISATION: N/A
FEAST DAY: 14 FEBRUARY
PATRONAGE: ARCHDIOCESE OF LJUBLJANA; EUROPE
ATTRIBUTES: BROTHERS DEPICTED TOGETHER

Cyril and Methodius were two brothers who converted many Slavs to Christianity, earning them the name 'Apostles to the Slavs'. After their deaths, their pupils continued their missionary work among other Slavs. In 1980, the first Slavic pope, Pope John Paul II, declared them co-patron saints of Europe, together with St Benedict. They are particularly venerated in Slovenia, where they are patron saints of the capital Ljubljana's archdiocese as well as Bulgaria. In the latter, the Order of Saints Cyril and Methodius is the national awards system, founded in 1909, and in 2021, a research vessel acquired by the Bulgarian Navy was re-christened SS Cyril and Methodius.

ST WENCESLAUS (AD c.907–929/935)

PLACE OF BIRTH: STOCHOV, CZECH REPUBLIC
DATE OF CANONISATION: N/A
FEAST DAY: 28 SEPTEMBER
PATRONAGE: PRAGUE, BOHEMIA, CZECH REPUBLIC
ATTRIBUTES: CROWN, DAGGER

Wenceslaus was the Duke of Bohemia and was assassinated by Boleslaus the Cruel, his martyrdom making him the patron saint of the Czech state. His grandfather, Borivoj I of Bohemia, was converted to Christianity by missionary brothers (and fellow saints) Cyril and Methodius, and Wenceslaus's faith was rewarded in battle when angels stood alongside him to force his enemy to back down. He was considered a saint immediately after his death, and a cult of Wenceslaus grew up in Bohemia and England. He is the subject of the Christmas carol Good King Wenceslas.

ST ADELAIDE (AD 931–999)

PLACE OF BIRTH: ORBE, SWITZERLAND

DATE OF CANONISATION: 1097

FEAST DAY: 16 DECEMBER

PATRONAGE: EMPRESSES

ATTRIBUTES: SCEPTRE AND CROWN

Adelaide was Holy Roman Empress by marriage to Otto the Great and was the first empress to share power with her husband. From a leading family herself, she was born in Orbe Castle to Rudolf II of Burgundy. She concerned herself greatly with the conversion of Slavic peoples to Christianity and the founding and restoring of monasteries, churches and abbeys. Towards the end of her days, she retired to a nunnery she had founded in Setz, Alsace. She died days short of the millennium, which she thought would bring the Second Coming of Christ.

ST HENRY II, HOLY ROMAN EMPEROR (AD 973–1024)

PLACE OF BIRTH: ABBACH, GERMANY

DATE OF CANONIZATION: 1146

FEAST DAY: 13 JULY

PATRONAGE: BASEL

ATTRIBUTES: KINGLY ROBES, CROWN

Henry, part of the Ottonian dynasty, was personally very pious and promoted the Church through his role, for which he was canonized by Pope Eugene III. He was celibate and he and his wife, the equally pious Cunigunde, had no children. He strongly enforced clerical celibacy. He had wished to become a monk, so the abbot of Verdun accepted him into his monastery but then ordered him to continue to administer the empire. The result of having such as pious emperor was that donations of riches and land to the Church grew under his rule, and the Church became increasingly part of the state. He donated the golden altar frontal in Basel Minster, Switzerland.

ST EDWARD (10TH–11TH CENTURY AD)

PLACE OF BIRTH: ISLIP, ENGLAND

DATE OF CANONIZATION: 1161

FEAST DAY: 13 OCTOBER

PATRONAGE: KINGS

ATTRIBUTES: CROWN

The last king of the House of Wessex, Edward the Confessor ruled England from 1042 until his death in 1066. The son of Ethelred the Unready, he succeeded his half-brother (and son of King Canute) Harthacnut. He was called the Confessor because he was pious and was regarded as a national saint of England until Edward III adopted St George. He was the only king of England to be canonized by the Pope. His shrine remains in Westminster Abbey, and the English monarch's crown – St Edward's Crown – is named after him.

AD
1000 – 1500

This period saw Christian knights travel from Europe to the Holy Land on the Crusades and the formation and expansion of many monastic orders, as well as early European settlement of the Americas. There are saints derived from all these enterprises.

ST MARGARET OF SCOTLAND (1045–1093)

PLACE OF BIRTH: HUNGARY

DATE OF CANONIZATION: 1250

FEAST DAY: 16 NOVEMBER

PATRONAGE: SCOTLAND

ATTRIBUTES: CROWN

Margaret is also known as Margaret of Wessex and was an English princess and a Scottish queen. Her father was Edward the Exile, who had been banished from Britain after King Canute had defeated his father, King Edmund Ironside, so Margaret was born in Hungary. Returning to Britain, she married Malcolm III of Scotland. Among her charitable works was the establishment of the ferry across the Firth of Forth for pilgrims travelling to St Andrews, which gave the towns of South Queensferry and North Queensferry their names. A devout woman, Margaret worked for the Church of Scotland to match the worship and practices of Rome and instigated the restoration of Iona Abbey.

ST BERNARD OF CLAIRVAUX (c.1090–1153)

PLACE OF BIRTH: FONTAINE-LES-DIJON, FRANCE

DATE OF CANONIZATION: 1174

FEAST DAY: 20 AUGUST

PATRONAGE: BURGUNDY, CISTERCIANS

ATTRIBUTES: CISTERCIAN HABIT, BOOK

A nobleman from Burgundy, Bernard of Clairvaux was a co-founder of the Knights Templar and a leader in the reformation of the Benedictine Order through its offshoot, the Cistercian Order. He joined the Cistercians – named after their abbey, at Citeaux – to live as they did, according to the Rule of St Benedict, along with 30 other noblemen from Burgundy. Many others followed Bernard, who then established his own abbey, which he called Clairvaux ('clear valley'). He then set up new communities. Later, Bernard embarked upon the Second Crusade. After it failed, he apologized to the Pope.

ST HEDWIG (1174–1243)

PLACE OF BIRTH: ANDECHS, GERMANY

DATE OF CANONIZATION: 1267

FEAST DAY: 16 OCTOBER

PATRONAGE: ANDECHS ABBEY, SILESIA

ATTRIBUTES: WEARING A CHURCH MODEL OR A PAIR OF SHOES IN HER HANDS

At the age of 12, Hedwig married Henry I the Bearded of Silesia, and on his death, he was buried at a Cistercian monastery of nuns he had established at Hedwig's request. Hedwig moved to the monastery, which was led by her daughter Gertrude, and assumed the religious habit of a lay sister. She invited numerous German religious people from the Holy Roman Empire to settle in the Silesian lands, now part of Poland. She forsook worldly goods and went barefoot, even in winter. When she was urged by the bishop of Wrocław to wear shoes, she carried them in her hands.

ST FRANCIS OF ASSISI (1181–1226)

PLACE OF BIRTH: ASSISI, ITALY

DATE OF CANONIZATION: 1228

FEAST DAY: 4 OCTOBER

PATRONAGE: POOR PEOPLE, ECOLOGY, MERCHANTS, ITALY

ATTRIBUTES: FRANCISCAN HABIT, BIRDS, ANIMALS, CRUCIFIX, BOOK, SKULL

Francis of Assisi was the founder of the Franciscans. As such, he is one of the most venerated figures in Christianity. He was inspired to live a life of poverty as an itinerant preacher. He travelled as far as Egypt, trying, in 1219, to convert the Sultan al-Kamil and put an end to the Fifth Crusade. He is said to have received the stigmata while praying, displaying the wounds of Christ. He is associated with the patronage of animals and the environment, and it became customary for churches to hold ceremonies blessing animals on his feast day.

SANCTA

ELISABETHA

ST ELIZABETH OF HUNGARY (1207–1231)

PLACE OF BIRTH: BRATISLAVA, SLOVAKIA

DATE OF CANONIZATION: 1235

FEAST DAY: 19 NOVEMBER

PATRONAGE: HOSPITALS

ATTRIBUTES: CROWN

Of royal birth, and the niece of St Hedwig of Andechs, Elizabeth was married at 14 but widowed at 20. She regained her dowry and used it to build a hospital, where she served the sick. Elizabeth was the daughter of King Andrew II of Hungary and, from 1223, she started to live according to the ideals of Francis of Assisi after she came into contact with Franciscan friars. One story about Elizabeth concerns a leper she laid in the bed she shared with her husband. When her husband heard of this, he was angry, but on lifting the bedclothes, he saw the figure of Christ on the Cross.

ST ZITA (1212–1272)

PLACE OF BIRTH: MONTE SAGRATI, ITALY

DATE OF CANONIZATION: 1696

FEAST DAY: 27 APRIL

PATRONAGE: MAIDS, DOMESTIC SERVANTS, LOST KEYS, WAITERS, WAITRESSES, LUCCA

ATTRIBUTES: KEYS

Zita, from near the city of Lucca, entered domestic service at the age of 12 and served the same family for almost 50 years. She gave a third of her wages to her parents, kept a third and gave the rest to the poor. The mistress of the house placed Zita in charge of almsgiving, and the maid was so devout she would rise several hours before the rest of the house each day to attend mass. Her body was exhumed more than three centuries after her death and was found to be incorrupt. It rests in the Basilica di San Frediano in Lucca. During the late medieval era, a cult around her grew in Europe. In England, she came to be known as Sitha and was invoked by servants who had lost their keys.

ST THOMAS AQUINAS (1225–1274)

PLACE OF BIRTH: ROCCASECCA, ITALY

DATE OF CANONIZATION: 1323

FEAST DAY: 28 JANUARY

PATRONAGE: AQUINO, ACADEMICS, CATHOLIC SCHOOLS

ATTRIBUTES: BOOK, A MODEL CHURCH

Thomas was born in Roccasecca, near the town of Aquino. His family wanted him to follow his uncle and join the Benedictine monastery at Monte Cassino. However, Thomas was set on joining the Dominican Order. Two of his brothers went as far as hiring a prostitute to seduce him to dissuade him from the Dominicans, but he drove her away with a burning log, with which he inscribed a cross on the wall. He went to Paris to study and then became a teacher and writer, with his ideas dominating much Catholic thinking and theology for centuries. He was a firm believer in social justice but also the death penalty.

ST GERTRUDE THE GREAT (1256–1302)

PLACE OF BIRTH: EISLEBEN, GERMANY
DATE OF CANONIZATION: 1677
FEAST DAY: 16 NOVEMBER
PATRONAGE: WEST INDIES
ATTRIBUTES: CROSS, RADIANT HEART

Gertrude entered the monastery school at Helfta, Germany, at the age of four. At 25, she had her first of a series of visions and started writing about Christianity. She saw herself as the Bride of Christ and was an early devotee of the Sacred Heart of Christ, in which Jesus's heart is seen as a symbol of God's love for humans. In the 17th century, King Philip IV of Spain, whose subjects had colonized much of the Caribbean, chose Gertrude to be the patron saint of the West Indies. In reference to her devotion to the Sacred Heart of Christ, she is often pictured with a heart in her hand, or it is displayed on her breast and surrounded by golden rays.

ST PEREGRINE LAZIOSI (1260–1345)

PLACE OF BIRTH: FORLI, ITALY

DATE OF CANONIZATION: 1726

FEAST DAY: 1 MAY

PATRONAGE: PATIENTS SUFFERING FROM CANCER,
AIDS AND OTHER LIFE-THREATENING ILLNESSES

ATTRIBUTES: ONE LEG COVERED IN A CANCEROUS SORE

Peregrine joined the Servite Order in Siena and went on to be ordained as a priest. He was then sent back to his home area where he founded a Servite house. It is said that Peregrine miraculously multiplied grain there, and people also took to calling him the 'Angel of Good Counsel' because of his sound advice. A penance he imposed on himself was to stand whenever he could sit, but at the age of 60, he developed an infection in his right leg. A doctor wanted to amputate it but, after a night in which Laziosi prayed before a fresco of the Crucifixion, the infection disappeared. Peregrine lived 25 years more.

ST ROCH (1295–1376/79)

PLACE OF BIRTH: MONTPELLIER, FRANCE

DATE OF CANONIZATION: N/A

FEAST DAY: 16 AUGUST

PATRONAGE: DOGS, INVALIDS, PILGRIMS, FALSELY ACCUSED PEOPLE

ATTRIBUTES: WOUND ON THIGH,

DOG OFFERING BREAD, PILGRIM'S STAFF

Known as Sao Roque in Portuguese, San Roque in Spanish and San Rocco in Italian, St Roch was born in the French city of Montpellier when it was part of the Kingdom of Majorca, and his mother had been barren until she prayed to the Virgin Mary. Roch was born with a red cross on his chest that grew as he did. In adulthood, he gave all his goods to the poor. He made a pilgrimage to Rome at a time of plague and found he was able to cure many people. Eventually, he fell ill himself, and the plague scarred his thigh, but a dog sustained him by carrying bread to him in its mouth. On his way back to Montpellier, he was arrested in the Italian town of Voghera and falsely accused of being a spy. He died in prison five years later.

ST BRIDGET OF SWEDEN (1303–1373)

PLACE OF BIRTH: UPPLAND, SWEDEN

DATE OF CANONIZATION: 1391

FEAST DAY: 23 JULY

PATRONAGE: EUROPE, SWEDEN, WIDOWS

ATTRIBUTES: PILGRIM'S HAT,

PILGRIM'S STAFF

Bridget was married at 13 and had eight children, but her husband died after the couple had returned from a pilgrimage to Santiago de Compostela. She subsequently devoted herself to a life of prayer and caring for the poor and sick, establishing the religious order of the Most Holy Saviour, which was to become known as the Bridgettines. A distinctive feature of the order at the time was that it comprised double monasteries, with men and women forming a joint community but living in separate cloisters. She also made pilgrimages to Rome and was made one of the six patron saints of Europe by Pope John Paul II in 1999.

ST CATHERINE OF SIENA (1347–1380)

PLACE OF BIRTH: SIENA, ITALY

DATE OF CANONIZATION: 1461

FEAST DAY: 29 APRIL

PATRONAGE: ROME, EUROPE

ATTRIBUTES: CRUCIFIX, BOOK,

MINIATURE SHIP BEARING PAPAL COAT OF ARMS

From an early age, Catherine, against the wishes of her parents, wanted to devote herself to God. She joined the 'mantellates', a group of pious women, primarily widows, and achieved some influence over Pope Gregory XI, playing a role in him leaving Avignon – where popes had been based for most of the 14th century – for Rome. He then sent her to negotiate peace with Florence, with which the papacy had been at war. In 1999, Pope John Paul II proclaimed her a co-patron saint of Europe.

ST LIDWINA (1380–1433)

PLACE OF BIRTH: SCHIEDAM, NETHERLANDS
DATE OF CANONIZATION: 1890
FEAST DAY: 14 APRIL
PATRONAGE: SCHIEDAM, CHRONIC PAIN, ICE SKATING
ATTRIBUTES: RECEIVING A BRANCH OF ROSES
AND A FLOWERING ROD FROM AN ANGEL

At 15, Lidwina had an ice-skating accident and became progressively disabled for the rest of her life. Despite this, Lidwina started fasting and found she had the ability to heal people, and there are many instances attesting to this. Lidwina's ailments may represent the first recorded case of multiple sclerosis – she developed walking difficulties and eventually became paralyzed. After she died, she was buried in a marble tomb, and her hometown of Schiedam became a place of pilgrimage.

ST RITA (1381–1457)

PLACE OF BIRTH: ROCCAPORENA, ITALY

DATE OF CANONIZATION: 1900

FEAST DAY: 22 MAY

PATRONAGE: ABUSED WIVES,
HEARTBROKEN WOMEN

ATTRIBUTES: FOREHEAD WOUND

Rita had an arranged marriage at the age of 12 to a nobleman called Paolo Mancini, who became abusive towards her. She had wanted to enter a convent. However, she converted her husband and after he died, she entered a monastery. In her latter years, she was meditating before an image of Christ on the Cross and a small wound appeared on her head, as though a thorn from Jesus's crown had penetrated her flesh. This was seen as partial stigmata, and she had this mark until her death. Even on occasions when she was exhumed, the wound was still fresh; as such, Rita was deemed 'incorruptible'.

ST COLETTE (1381–1447)
PLACE OF BIRTH: CORBIE, FRANCE
DATE OF CANONIZATION: 1807
FEAST DAY: 6 MARCH
PATRONAGE: WOMEN SEEKING TO CONCEIVE, EXPECTANT MOTHERS
ATTRIBUTES: N/A

Colette was the foundress of the Colettine Poor Clares, a reform branch of the Order of Saint Clare better known as the Poor Clares. It is said that her mother gave birth to her at age 60 after she and her husband prayed to St Nicholas for help in having a child. Out of gratitude, they named the baby after the saint, calling her Nicolette, which was shortened to Colette. After time with the Beguines, the Benedictines and the Franciscans, she joined the Poor Clares, and Antipope Benedict XIII of Avignon, who was recognized in France as the rightful pope at the time, authorized her to reform the order. She subsequently founded 18 monasteries for the order, where she prescribed extreme poverty and going barefoot. While travelling to meet Benedict, she stayed with a friend whose wife was having a difficult labour. The woman credited Colette's prayers with the successful birth.

ST JOAN OF ARC (c.1412–1431)

PLACE OF BIRTH: DOMREMY, FRANCE

DATE OF CANONIZATION: 1920

FEAST DAY: 30 MAY

PATRONAGE: FRANCE

ATTRIBUTES: WITH SWORD, IN ARMOUR, WITH CROSS, AT THE STAKE

Joan of Arc is a patron saint of France, honoured as a defender of the French nation in the Hundred Years War. Although only a teenager and from a peasant background, she had requested to be taken to Charles VII of France, saying that she could help him defeat the English. She claimed that visions of angels and saints had guided her. Having faith in her, Charles sent her to Orleans, where she helped the French defend the city. Eventually, she was taken by the English and burned at the stake. She has become a feminist icon for being a military leader when that was a male preserve, as well as for adopting men's clothing. She has also been a source of inspiration for much drama and music.

ST VERONICA OF MILAN (1445–1497)

PLACE OF BIRTH: BINASCO, ITALY

DATE OF CANONIZATION: 1672

FEAST DAY: 13 JANUARY

PATRONAGE: BINASCO

ATTRIBUTES: WITH A VISION OF THE VIRGIN MARY

Veronica was from a poor family and saw frequent visions of the Virgin Mary. On one occasion, when she received a vision of Christ, he gave her a message for Pope Alexander VI, and she travelled to Rome to deliver it. As a nun of the Augustinian Order (following the Rule of St Augustine of Hippo) she tried to teach herself to read. However, as she was doing so, she was visited by the Virgin Mary, who told her that reading was not necessary. However, she said, three things were: purity of intention, abhorrence of criticism and daily meditation on Christ's suffering. She died on the date she predicted: 13 January 1497.

ST CASIMIR (1458–1484)

PLACE OF BIRTH: KRAKÓW, POLAND

DATE OF CANONIZATION: 1521

FEAST DAY: 4 MARCH

PATRONAGE: LITHUANIA

ATTRIBUTES: GRAND DUCAL CAP

A son of King Casimir IV Jagiellon of Poland, who was also Grand Duke of Lithuania, Casimir was born in Wawel Castle in Kraków. His mother, Queen Elisabeth Habsburg of Austria, took an active interest in her children's upbringing and the family often accompanied the king on his trips to Lithuania. A pious man who died of tuberculosis at only 25, Casimir could often be found, pre-dawn, kneeling by church gates waiting for the priest to open them, and it is said his lung condition may have been brought on by a particularly hard fast. When Lithuania was being besieged by the army of the Grand Duchy of Moscow in 1518, it is believed St Casimir appeared before troops and showed them where they could safely cross the Daugava River.

ST JUAN DIEGO (1474–1548)

PLACE OF BIRTH: CUAUTITLÁN, MEXICO

DATE OF CANONIZATION: 2002

FEAST DAY: 9 DECEMBER

PATRONAGE: INDIGENOUS PEOPLE

ATTRIBUTES: CLOAK CONTAINING AN IMAGE OF THE VIRGIN MARY

St Juan Diego is the first saint indigenous to the Americas. From the Nahua peoples, Juan Diego is said to have been visited by the Virgin Mary on four occasions in December 1531, the final time in front of Juan de Zumarraga, then bishop of Mexico. The Basilica of Our Lady of Guadalupe, at the foot of the hill where Juan Diego had the first three visions, houses the cloak imprinted with an image of the Virgin Mary from those visitations. As a result, the basilica has become a major pilgrimage destination, receiving 22 million visitors in 2010 alone. It was Pope John Paul II who, in 1990, beatified Juan Diego, and then later canonized him, travelling to Mexico both times to preside over the ceremonies.

ST ANGELA MERICI (1474–1540)

PLACE OF BIRTH: DESENZANO DEL GARDA, ITALY

DATE OF CANONIZATION: 1807

FEAST DAY: 27 JANUARY

PATRONAGE: LOSS OF PARENTS, COURAGE, STRENGTH, DETERMINATION

ATTRIBUTES: CLOAK

Angela Merici founded the Company of St Ursula, in which women dedicated their lives to the Church through the education of girls. From this organization sprang the monastic Order of Saint Ursula. Orphaned with her older sister at 10 years old, Angela had a vision that she was to found an association of virgins who were to devote their lives to the training of young girls. She was struck blind on the island of Crete while travelling to the Holy Land, but was cured on her return by praying at a crucifix at the same spot where she had lost her sight.

ST IGNATIUS LOYOLA (1491–1556)

PLACE OF BIRTH: AZPEITIA, SPAIN

DATE OF CANONIZATION: 1622

FEAST DAY: 31 JULY

PATRONAGE: SOCIETY OF JESUS, ACCIDENTS AND INJURIES

ATTRIBUTES: CASSOCK

Spanish priest Ignatius Loyola, along with six companions, founded the Society of Jesus, better known as the Jesuits. As well as vows of chastity, obedience and poverty common to other Catholic orders, he added obedience to the Pope. As such, Jesuits were instrumental in leading the Counter-Reformation in response to the emergence of Protestantism. He started adult life as a womanizing soldier with a penchant for fancy dressing but converted to Christianity while recovering from several leg operations after a cannonball shattered his right leg. As a result, this leg was shorter than the left for the rest of his life and he walked with a limp. After the foundation of the Jesuits, he was chosen as its first Superior General and presided over the foundation of many schools, colleges and seminaries across Europe.

ST JOHN OF GOD (1495–1550)

PLACE OF BIRTH: MONTEMOR-O-NOVO, PORTUGAL

DATE OF CANONIZATION: 1690

FEAST DAY: 8 MARCH

PATRONAGE: HOSPITALS, THE SICK

ATTRIBUTES: ALMS

John was a soldier who took to looking after the sick, and his followers formed the Brothers Hospitallers of Saint John of God, dedicated to caring for the poor and ill. The order, which was approved by the Holy See in 1572, has been officially entrusted with the medical care of the Pope and operates in 53 countries. John converted to Christianity after seeing a vision of the infant Jesus, who gave him the name John of God. He then devoted himself to the needs of others and began working with the poor, spurred on by a vision of the Virgin Mary. He died in Granada from pneumonia after jumping into a river to save a young man.

AD
1500 – 2000

As Europeans colonised regions far and wide, they
took Christianity with them, and, consequently, there
are now saints from all four corners of the globe.
Meanwhile, the advent of photography meant that the
attributes of saints became less significant.

ST TERESA OF AVILA (1515–1582)

PLACE OF BIRTH: AVILA, SPAIN

DATE OF CANONIZATION: 1622

FEAST DAY: 15 OCTOBER

PATRONAGE: SPAIN

ATTRIBUTES: CARMELITE RELIGIOUS HABIT

Teresa of Avila was a Carmelite nun and religious reformer. She felt that spiritual practice at her convent had lost its purpose because of the daily invasion of visitors, many of high social and political rank, so she founded a new convent and received a papal sanction for her primary principles of absolute poverty and renunciation of ownership of property. She established a number of reformed convents, and, with Carmelite friar John of the Cross, she formed the Discalced Carmelites order. 'Discalced' derives from the Latin for 'without shoes'. In 1970, Pope Paul VI proclaimed her the first female Doctor of the Church.

ST PHILIP NERI (1515–1595)

PLACE OF BIRTH: FLORENCE, ITALY

DATE OF CANONIZATION: 1622

FEAST DAY: 26 MAY

PATRONAGE: ROME, ITALY

ATTRIBUTES: N/A

Philip was a priest who founded the Congregation of the Oratory, a society of secular clergy. In the Congregation, Catholic priests and lay brothers live together in a community bound together but without formal vows. The Oratory movement spread quickly in Italy and France. Before Philip became a priest, he did much charity work in Rome. Ministering to the sick, poor and prostitutes, he gathered a number of disciples, many of whom became Jesuits, as Philip knew the founder, Ignatius Loyola. He then ministered to the needs of the thousands of pilgrims who flocked to Rome each year. Much of his success is attributed to his friendly and joyful character. He is said to have been a man of good humour, and the organization he founded has established Oratories around the world.

TORIBIO DE MOGROVEJO (1538–1606)

PLACE OF BIRTH: MAYORGA DE CAMPOS, SPAIN

DATE OF CANONIZATION: 1726

FEAST DAY: 23 MARCH

PATRONAGE: PERU, LIMA, LATIN AMERICAN BISHOPS, NATIVE PEOPLES

ATTRIBUTES: EPISCOPAL CLOTHING

Toribio was archbishop of Lima in Peru from 1579 until his death and achieved the position through his piety rather than any government or judicial experience. Born in Spain, he set off on his mission to Peru after being ordained and he baptized many Native Peruvians. He is said to have confirmed nearly half a million people, including St Martin de Porres. He also built roads, schools, chapels and hospitals, and founded the first seminary in the Western Hemisphere. It is claimed that he predicted the exact date and hour of his death.

ST CHARLES BORROMEO (1538–1584)

PLACE OF BIRTH: ARONA, ITALY

DATE OF CANONIZATION: 1610

FEAST DAY: 4 NOVEMBER

PATRONAGE: BISHOPS, SEMINARIES

ATTRIBUTES: ROBES, BAREFOOT, CARRYING THE CROSS AS AN ARCHBISHOP

Charles Borromeo, an archbishop of Milan, was a leading figure, along with Ignatius Loyola and Philip Neri, in the Counter-Reformation. He was concerned with priests who were lazy or poorly educated, so he established seminaries, colleges and communities for their training. He also reformed the Archdiocese of Milan, the largest in Italy at the time, with 800,000 people and 3000 clergy. The selling of ecclesiastic positions had become rife, with art with little scriptural foundation finding its way into churches. Charles was canonized for helping to restore the reputation of the Church.

ST JOHN OF THE CROSS (1542–1591)

PLACE OF BIRTH: FONTIVEROS, SPAIN

DATE OF CANONIZATION: 1726

FEAST DAY: 14 DECEMBER

PATRONAGE: SPANISH POETS

ATTRIBUTES: CARMELITE HABIT,

QUILL

John of the Cross was a Spanish Carmelite friar who helped to reform the Carmelite Order with Teresa of Avila, to try to restore it to the purity of its origins. After studying theology and philosophy at the University of Salamanca, he had considered joining the Carthusian Order, its practice of silent and solitary contemplation appealing to him. With Teresa, he established a new monastery for Carmelite friars at Duruelo, then named himself 'St John of the Cross'. John was also a writer who was considered one of the foremost poets in Spanish.

ST MARTIN DE PORRES (1579–1639)

PLACE OF BIRTH: LIMA, PERU

DATE OF CANONIZATION: 1962

FEAST DAY: 3 NOVEMBER

PATRONAGE: MIXED-RACE PEOPLE, ANIMALS

ATTRIBUTES: A DOG, A CAT,

A BIRD AND A MOUSE EATING TOGETHER FROM THE SAME DISH, A BROOM

Martin de Porres was the illegitimate son of a Spanish nobleman and a woman of African and native Peruvian descent. Under Peruvian law, descendants of Africans and Native Americans were forbidden from becoming full members of religious orders, so the pious Martin asked the Dominicans at Holy Rosary Priory in Lima if he could be a *donado* – a volunteer who performed menial tasks in the monastery in return for being able to wear the habit and live as part of the community. Ultimately, he was permitted to become a lay brother and was put in charge of the infirmary. Martin did not eat meat, and among the many miracles attributed to him was an ability to communicate with animals. He also appears as a character in the video for Madonna's song 'Like a Prayer'.

ST VINCENT DE PAUL (1581–1660)

PLACE OF BIRTH: POUY, FRANCE
DATE OF CANONIZATION: 1737
FEAST DAY: 27 SEPTEMBER
PATRONAGE: CHARITIES, HOSPITALS,
PRISONERS
ATTRIBUTES: WITH A CHILD IN HIS ARMS

It is claimed that while sailing along the south coast of France in a boat as a student of theology, Vincent de Paul was captured by pirates and taken to Tunis, where he was auctioned off as a slave. He was freed two years later, after being passed between various owners. On his return to Europe, he gathered money to release galley slaves in North Africa and then founded the Congregation of the Mission Society. The priests within the society swore vows of poverty, chastity and obedience, and devoted themselves to serving people in smaller towns and villages. He also founded the Daughters of Charity of Saint Vincent de Paul, a society for Catholic women through which they could serve the poor. Due to his dedication to charity, he is often portrayed with a child in his arms.

ST ROSE OF LIMA (1586–1617)

PLACE OF BIRTH: LIMA, PERU
DATE OF CANONIZATION: 1671
FEAST DAY: 23 AUGUST
PATRONAGE: EMBROIDERY, GARDENING,
CULTIVATION OF BLOOMING FLOWERS, PERU, THE AMERICAS
ATTRIBUTES: ROSES

Rose of Lima is known for her life of severe penance and care for the poverty-stricken of Lima. As a young girl, she took to fasting three times a week and, when older and admired for her beauty, she cut off her hair and rubbed pepper in her face. Her parents wanted her to marry, but she took a vow of virginity. Later, she restricted herself to two hours of sleep a night so she could devote as much time as possible to prayer. She sold her embroidery and the flowers she had grown so she could help her family and give to the poor, and, for her piety and charitable works, she was the first person born in the Americas to be canonized. She was named Isabel at birth. However, when she was a child, a servant claimed to see her face transform into a rose, so she was given that moniker.

ST LORENZO RUIZ (1594–1637)

PLACE OF BIRTH: MANILA, PHILIPPINES
DATE OF CANONIZATION: 1987
FEAST DAY: 28 SEPTEMBER
PATRONAGE: PHILIPPINES, FILIPINOS OVERSEAS,
CHINESE FILIPINOS
ATTRIBUTES: GALLOWS AND PIT, PALM OF MARTYRDOM

Lorenzo Ruiz was born in Manila to a Chinese father and a Filipino mother. After being educated by Dominicans and marrying, he was falsely accused of killing a Spaniard. Lorenzo sought asylum on board a ship with three Dominican priests, and they sailed to Okinawa, Japan, where Christians were being persecuted. There, they were thrown into prison and taken to Nagasaki, where they were tortured and hung upside down over a pit. Despite his suffering, Lorenzo refused to recant Christianity. He died two days later, and his martyrdom was witnessed by two Japanese ex-Jesuit priests. Lorenzo was beatified during Pope John Paul II's visit to the Philippines in 1981, the first beatification held outside the Vatican. He was canonized by the same pope as the first Filipino saint.

ST JOSEPH OF CUPERTINO (1603–1663)

PLACE OF BIRTH: CUPERTINO, ITALY

DATE OF CANONIZATION: 1767

FEAST DAY: 18 SEPTEMBER

PATRONAGE: CUPERTINO, AVIATION,

ASTRONAUTS, MENTAL HANDICAPS

ATTRIBUTES: LEVITATING

According to Franciscan accounts, Joseph was 'remarkably unclever', and the visions he received throughout his life made him the object of scorn. He applied to join the Conventual Franciscan friars but was rejected due to his lack of education, so he pleaded with them to let him work in their stables. He so impressed the friars with his work there that they admitted him to their Order, and he became a priest, living a strictly ascetic life. He was reported to be able to levitate, and, as this was seen as connected to witchcraft, his superiors confined him to a cell. He lived under the supervision of other priests in his later years.

ST MARIANA OF JESUS PAREDES (1618–1645)

PLACE OF BIRTH: QUITO, ECUADOR

DATE OF CANONIZATION: 1950

FEAST DAY: 26 MAY

PATRONAGE: ECUADOR

ATTRIBUTES: LILY

Mariana was the first person to be canonized from what is now Ecuador. A recluse, she is said to have sacrificed herself for her city, Quito. She was allowed to live an ascetic lifestyle as a reclusive, spiritual child at home, refusing to enter a monastery. Her dealings with the outside world were confined to a nearby Jesuit church. In 1645, Quito suffered earthquakes and subsequent epidemics, during which Mariana publicly offered herself as a victim for the city. She died shortly afterwards, and it is said that immediately after her death, a pure white lily sprang up from her blood and bloomed.

ST KATERI TEKAKWITHA (1656–1680)

PLACE OF BIRTH: OSSERNENON, USA

DATE OF CANONIZATION: 2012

FEAST DAY: 17 APRIL

PATRONAGE: LOSS OF PARENTS, PEOPLE IN EXILE, NATIVE AMERICANS

ATTRIBUTES: LILY, CROSS

Kateri Tekakwitha was a Native American born in what is modern-day New York State. She converted to Catholicism at age 19, took a vow of perpetual virginity – despite pressure from her extended family to marry – and moved to a Jesuit mission in Quebec. Both her parents had died of smallpox; she survived but had facial scars and impaired eyesight. Over the centuries, opinion spread that Kateri – known informally as Lily of the Mohawks, as the lily was seen as a symbol of purity – should be recognized as a saint. Kateri, who has a number of miracles attributed to her, was finally beatified by Pope John Paul II in 1980 and canonized by Pope Benedict XVI in 2012.

S. ALPHONSO DE LIGORIO PATRITIO NEAPOLITANO
EPO SANCTAGATENSI CONG. SS. RED. FVNDATORI
COLLEGIVM BENEVENTANV ANNO. D. MDCCLXXVII.

ST ALPHONSUS LIGUORI (1696–1787)

PLACE OF BIRTH: MARIANELLA, ITALY

DATE OF CANONIZATION: 1839

FEAST DAY: 1 AUGUST

PATRONAGE: NAPLES,

LAWYERS

ATTRIBUTES: PRAYING

Multi-talented Alphonsus was a bishop, composer, musician, artist, poet, lawyer and philosopher, who also founded the Congregation of the Most Holy Redeemer, known as the Redemptionists. He was from a military family, but poor eyesight and asthma precluded the same line of work for him, so he studied law. Alphonsus became a successful lawyer but was called to the priesthood. Once ordained, he lived among the homeless and marginalized in Naples and established the Congregation of the Most Holy Redeemer to serve them. He used his skills with music and words to write hymns and taught them to people in his parish missions. He was ultimately appointed bishop of Sant'Agata de' Goti in the Campania region.

ST JUNIPERO SERRA (1713–1784)

PLACE OF BIRTH: PETRA, MAJORCA

DATE OF CANONIZATION: 2015

FEAST DAY: 28 AUGUST

PATRONAGE: HISPANIC AMERICANS, CALIFORNIA

ATTRIBUTES: FRANCISCAN HABIT,

ACCOMPANIED BY A YOUNG NATIVE AMERICAN BOY

Junipero Serra was a Spanish priest and missionary who is credited with establishing the Franciscan missions in the Sierra Gorda in modern-day Mexico, now a UNESCO World Heritage Site. He also founded a mission in Mexico's Baja California, as well as eight of the 21 Spanish missions in what is now the USA between San Diego and San Francisco. For this, he is known as the 'Apostle of California', although he has been criticized for alleged mandatory conversions to Catholicism and abuse of Native American converts. He died in Carmel, California.

ST FELIX OF NICOSIA (1715–1787)

PLACE OF BIRTH: NICOSIA, ITALY
DATE OF CANONIZATION: 2005
FEAST DAY: 2 JUNE
PATRONAGE: N/A
ATTRIBUTES: CAPUCHIN'S HABIT

Felix tried several times over eight years to be accepted at a Capuchin friary but was repeatedly rejected, his cause not helped by his being illiterate. However, the friars were impressed by his perseverance, and he was finally accepted. He had a gift for healing, which he utilized when an epidemic started decimating the Sicilian town of Cerami in March 1777. Ten years later, he was overtaken by a raging fever while working in the garden. A doctor prescribed medicines, but Felix told the physician that they would prove useless, as this would be his final illness. He died later that month.

ST MARY FRANCES OF THE FIVE WOUNDS (1715–1791)

PLACE OF BIRTH: NAPLES, SICILY

DATE OF CANONIZATION: 1867

FEAST DAY: 6 OCTOBER

PATRONAGE: THE QUARTIERI SPAGNOLI OF NAPLES

ATTRIBUTES: CROSS, WOUNDS ON HANDS

St Mary Frances of the Five Wounds was born Anna Maria Gallo in the Quartieri Spagnoli (Spanish Quarter) of Naples, which was known as the red-light district, and gained her saintly name because she received the stigmata. Her father had wanted her to marry, but she was determined to join the Franciscan Order and lead a religious life helping others while living in the family home. To cover her wounds, she would often wear gloves. The residents of the Quartieri Spagnoli credit her with the limited damage that occurred to the area in World War II when more than 100 bombs were dropped on it.

ST GERARD MAJELLA (1726–1755)

PLACE OF BIRTH: MURO LUCANO, ITALY

DATE OF CANONIZATION: 1904

FEAST DAY: 16 OCTOBER

PATRONAGE: CHILDREN, UNBORN CHILDREN, MOTHERS, EXPECTANT MOTHERS,
MOTHERHOOD, LAY BROTHERS

ATTRIBUTES: YOUNG MAN IN A REDEMPTORIST HABIT

Gerard was a lay brother with the Congregation of the Most
Holy Redeemer and is credited with many miracles. He is said
to have restored life to a boy who had fallen off a cliff, to have
made a scant supply of wheat last until the next harvest, and
to have multiplied the bread he was distributing to the poor.
One day, he walked across stormy water to lead a boatload of
fishermen to the shore. A handkerchief he gave to a girl was
credited years later as being the object that helped her safely
deliver a baby as the mother neared death in childbirth.

ST ELIZABETH ANN SETON (1774–1821)

PLACE OF BIRTH: NEW YORK CITY

DATE OF CANONIZATION: 1975

FEAST DAY: 4 JANUARY

PATRONAGE: CATHOLIC SCHOOLS,

WIDOWS

ATTRIBUTES: N/A

The founder of the United States' Catholic parochial school system, Elizabeth Ann Seton became the first person born in what would become the USA to be canonized. Widowed at an early age, she established Saint Joseph's Academy and Free School in Emmitsburg, Maryland, which was dedicated to girls' education. She then established a religious community in Emmitsburg for the care of poor children. This was the start of the US Catholic parochial school system. After her death, the Sisters of Charity of St Joseph's established more schools.

ST CATHERINE LABOURE (1806–1876)

PLACE OF BIRTH: FAIN-LES-MOUTIERS, FRANCE
DATE OF CANONIZATION: 1947
FEAST DAY: 28 NOVEMBER
PATRONAGE: SENIORS
ATTRIBUTES: MIRACULOUS MEDAL

Catherine Laboure is believed to have relayed the request from the Virgin Mary to create the Miraculous Medal of Our Lady of Graces, worn by millions of people around the world. Laboure also spent 40 years caring for the aged and infirm. Her mother died when she was nine, and it is said that after the funeral, Laboure picked up a statue of the Virgin Mary, kissed it and said, 'Now you will be my mother.' She joined a convent in Paris, where it is said she received a request from the Virgin Mary to create the medallions along with guidance on the visions to put on them.

ST AMBROSE OF OPTINA (1812–1891)

PLACE OF BIRTH: BOLSHAYA LIPOVITSA, RUSSIA

DATE OF CANONIZATION: 1988

FEAST DAY: 23 OCTOBER

PATRONAGE: N/A

ATTRIBUTES: CLOTHED AS A MONK, SOMETIMES HOLDING A SCROLL

Shortly before graduation from clerical school, Ambrose became severely ill and made a vow that if he got well, he would become a monk. He duly did, at the Optina Monastery in Kaluga, where he became the principal elder for 30 years despite still being afflicted by ill health. Ambrose was indefatigable in counselling people and is also said to have had the gift of being able to see into people's souls, where no secret was hidden, along with clairvoyance and healing. However, he was modest, so he tried to conceal the latter. In 1884, Ambrose founded the Shamordino Convent, which took in women who were poor, sick and blind.

ANDREW KIM TAEGON (1821–1846)

PLACE OF BIRTH: SOLMOU, KOREA

DATE OF CANONIZATION: 1984

FEAST DAY: 20 SEPTEMBER

PATRONAGE: KOREAN CLERGY

ATTRIBUTES: N/A

Andrew was the first Korean-born Catholic priest. He was from a Catholic family, the denomination having taken hold in certain communities after Korean scholars visiting China brought back Western books that had been translated into Chinese. Andrew's father was, in fact, a martyr, as practising Christianity – although done by some – was prohibited at the time. Andrew studied in the Portuguese colony of Macau. He was ordained as a priest in Shanghai and then returned to Korea to preach. Ultimately, Andrew was martyred when, at 25, he was tortured and beheaded.

ST DAMIEN OF MOLOKAI (1840–1889)

PLACE OF BIRTH: TREMELO, BELGIUM

DATE OF CANONIZATION: 2009

FEAST DAY: 10 MAY

PATRONAGE: LEPERS, OUTCASTS, HAWAII

ATTRIBUTES: HAT, SORES

Praying every day at the Fathers of the Sacred Heart of Jesus and Mary in Belgium to be sent on a mission, Damien's wish was granted when he was sent to Hawaii. There, he is recognized for his ministry to people with leprosy, but after 11 years of caring for the physical, spiritual and emotional needs of those in the colony on the island of Molokai, he contracted leprosy himself. Damien continued his work despite having the disease and eventually succumbed to it. The day of his death, 15 April, is a state-wide holiday in Hawaii.

ST DOMINIC SAVIO (1842–1857)

PLACE OF BIRTH: SAN GIOVANNI, ITALY

DATE OF CANONIZATION: 1954

FEAST DAY: 6 MAY

PATRONAGE: CHOIRBOYS

ATTRIBUTES: BOOK

Dominic Savio was studying to be a priest when he became ill and died at the age of 14. He was noted for his piety and devotion to the Catholic faith and was canonized by Pope Pius XII in 1954, who described him as 'small in size, but a towering giant in spirit'. His tutor, John Bosco, wrote a biography of the boy. Dominic could pray by the age of four and would often be found doing so alone. If he turned up before the church opened, he would kneel and pray outside it, even in mud and snow. At the age of five, he learned to serve mass.

ST BERNADETTE (1844–1879)

PLACE OF BIRTH: LOURDES, FRANCE

DATE OF CANONIZATION: 1933

FEAST DAY: 16 APRIL

PATRONAGE: LOURDES

ATTRIBUTES: N/A

In 1858, Bernadette Soubirous, a miller's daughter, experienced an apparition of the Virgin Mary, who asked for a chapel to be built in a cave near her home in Lourdes. She went on to join the Sisters of Charity of Nevers at their convent, and since her death, her body has been deemed to have remained internally incorrupt. The grotto where the apparitions occurred has become a major pilgrimage site, and a Marian shrine known as the Sanctuary of Our Lady of Lourdes attracts around five million pilgrims a year.

ST CLELIA BARBIERI (1847–1870)

PLACE OF BIRTH: LE BUDRIE, ITALY
DATE OF CANONIZATION: 1989
FEAST DAY: 13 JULY
PATRONAGE: LITTLE SISTERS OF THE MOTHER OF SORROWS
ATTRIBUTES: EYES LOOKING TO HEAVEN

Clelia was the founder of the Little Sisters of the Mother of
Sorrows and is regarded as the youngest founder of a religious
congregation in the history of the Catholic Church. She joined
the Workers of the Christian Catechism as an assistant teacher
in 1861 and became such an inspirational teacher that the
parish priest entrusted her with the teaching and guidance
of girls in doctrine. At 21, she formed the Little Sisters but
died at 23 from tuberculosis. At a younger age, she declined
married life, even when pressured, to dedicate her life to the
needs of others.

ST FRANCES XAVIER CABRINI (1850–1917)

PLACE OF BIRTH: SANT'ANGELO LODIGIANO, ITALY

DATE OF CANONIZATION: 1946

FEAST DAY: 13 NOVEMBER

PATRONAGE: IMMIGRANTS

ATTRIBUTES: N/A

Frances founded the Missionary Sisters of the Sacred Heart of Jesus (MSC), which played a large role in Italian immigrants settling in the United States. She was the first US citizen to be canonized. In 1880, with seven other women who had taken religious vows, she founded the MSC in the northern Italian province of Lodi. In 1887, she asked the Pope if she could establish missions to China. Instead, he urged her to go to the United States, where Italian immigrants were flocking, mostly in great poverty. She arrived in New York City and founded 67 missionary institutions to serve the sick and poor, not just in the USA. She was naturalized as a US citizen in 1909.

ST THERESE OF LISIEUX (1873–1897)

PLACE OF BIRTH: ALENÇON, FRANCE

DATE OF CANONIZATION: 1925

FEAST DAY: 1 OCTOBER

PATRONAGE: ILLNESSES, FRANCE

ATTRIBUTES: DISCALCED CARMELITE HABIT

Therese was a Discalced Carmelite nun known in English as the Little Flower of Jesus. Although she was obscure during her lifetime, Pope Pius X called her 'the greatest saint of modern times'. She is seen as the model of sanctity and is known for her spiritual memoir, *Story of a Soul*. She died of tuberculosis at 24 and is widely venerated. After Lourdes, the Basilica of Lisieux – dedicated to St Therese – is the most popular pilgrimage destination in France, and in 1944 Pope Pius XII decreed her a co-patron of France along with Joan of Arc. In 1997, Pope John Paul II made her the youngest Doctor of the Church.

LAURA MONTOYA (1874–1949)

PLACE OF BIRTH: JENCO, COLOMBIA

DATE OF CANONIZATION: 2013

FEAST DAY: 21 OCTOBER

PATRONAGE: PEOPLE WHO SUFFER FROM RACIAL DISCRIMINATION

ATTRIBUTES: RELIGIOUS HABIT

Laura was the founder of the Congregation of the Missionary Sisters of the Immaculate Virgin Mary and Saint Catherine of Siena. She was lauded for her work with indigenous peoples and for acting as a role model for South American girls. The first Colombian to become a saint, she founded her congregation to spread the gospel among the indigenous peoples of her region, for which she went to live in the town of Dabeiba. The last nine years of her life were lived in a wheelchair because of a prolonged illness, and she died in the city of Medellin, where her tomb is located.

ST MARIA GUADALUPE GARCIA ZAVALA (1878–1963)

PLACE OF BIRTH: ZAPOPAN, MEXICO

DATE OF CANONIZATION: 2013

FEAST DAY: 24 JUNE

PATRONAGE: NURSES,

HANDMAIDS OF ANTA MARGHERITA MARIA AND THE POOR

ATTRIBUTES: RELIGIOUS HABIT

This Mexican sister co-founded the Handmaids of Santa Margherita and the Poor. She had been engaged to be married but called it off to follow her religious calling and care for ill people. At times, she would beg in the street for funds to care for the sick but would not take more than what was needed. During the Mexican Revolution, priests were hunted down, and she hid them along with the archbishop of Guadalajara in her hospital. Her order has spread to places as widespread as Iceland and Peru, and in 2015 it was present in 22 locations.

ST PADRE PIO (1887–1968)

PLACE OF BIRTH: PIETRELCINA, ITALY

DATE OF CANONIZATION: 2002

FEAST DAY: 23 SEPTEMBER

PATRONAGE: CIVIL DEFENCE VOLUNTEERS,
ADOLESCENTS

ATTRIBUTES: STIGMATA, FRANCISCAN HABIT

Padre Pio was marked by stigmata in 1918 and attracted many followers to San Giovanni Rotondo, where he was a Franciscan Capuchin priest. He was also the founder of the nearby Casa Sollievo della Sofferenza hospital. Pio, who had been deemed too frail to be conscripted, was seen as a symbol of hope for people rebuilding their lives after World War I. In 1968, a mass and a large crowd of pilgrims (including television crews) marked the fiftieth anniversary of Pio receiving the stigmata. The next day, he made his last confession and renewed his Franciscan vows. He then died, and a doctor revealed that his stigmata wounds had healed without any trace of a scar.

ST MARIA GORETTI (1890–1902)

PLACE OF BIRTH: CORINALDO, ITALY

DATE OF CANONIZATION: 1950

FEAST DAY: 6 JULY

PATRONAGE: FORGIVENESS AND MERCY, VICTIMS OF RAPE, CRIME VICTIMS, TEENAGERS

ATTRIBUTES: FARMER'S CLOTHING, MARTYR'S PALM

Maria was martyred as a virgin when she was stabbed 14 times after she refused to submit to the sexual advances of a 20-year-old, Alessandro, with whom her poor farming family were sharing a house. She died in hospital after forgiving him. Alessandro was imprisoned for 27 years, and on his release, he begged Maria's mother for forgiveness, which she granted. He became a lay brother in a Capuchin monastery. During her ordeal, Maria, then aged 11, had told Alessandro that what he wanted was a mortal sin, and as she was being treated, ultimately unsuccessfully, for her wounds, she forgave him and said she wanted to see him in Heaven.

ST TERESIA BENEDICTA A CRUCE (1891–1942)

PLACE OF BIRTH: WROCŁAW, POLAND

DATE OF CANONIZATION: 1998

FEAST DAY: 9 AUGUST

PATRONAGE: EUROPE, CONVERTED JEWS, MARTYRS

ATTRIBUTES: DISCALCED CARMELITE NUN'S HABIT, SOMETIMES WITH A YELLOW STAR, BOOK OR SCROLL WITH HEBREW LETTERS

Born Edith Stein, St Teresia was a German Jew who converted to Christianity and became a Discalced Carmelite nun and philosopher. From reading about the reformer of the Carmelite Order, Teresa of Avila, she was drawn to the Christian faith. She was baptized into the Catholic Church in 1922 and became a teacher in a Catholic school. However, because of the Nazi requirement of an 'Aryan certificate' for civil servants from 1933, she had to leave her teaching position. She entered a Discalced Carmelite monastery and took the name Teresia Benedicta a Cruce. As the persecution of Jews – even those who had converted to Christianity – intensified, she moved to a Carmelite monastery in the Netherlands but was captured by the Nazis, taken to Auschwitz and gassed on 9 August 1942.

ST MAXIMILIAN KOLBE (1894–1941)

PLACE OF BIRTH: ZDURISKA WOLA, POLAND
DATE OF CANONIZATION: 1982
FEAST DAY: 14 AUGUST
PATRONAGE: AMATEUR RADIO OPERATORS
ATTRIBUTES: FRANCISCAN HABIT, NAZI CONCENTRATION CAMP BADGE

Maximilian volunteered to die in place of a Polish army sergeant called Franciszek Gajowniczek in the German death camp Auschwitz. Gajowniczek would live until 1995; Maximilian died from a lethal injection at Auschwitz on 14 August 1941. Maximilian had been a Conventual Franciscan friar who founded and supervised the Polish monastery of Niepokalanow. He also ran an amateur radio station. During World War II, he refused to sign the Deutsche Volksliste, which would have given him rights similar to those of German citizens because of his ethnic German ancestry. He was later arrested by the Gestapo and taken to Auschwitz.

ST THERESA OF LOS ANDES (1900–1920)

PLACE OF BIRTH: SANTIAGO, CHILE
DATE OF CANONIZATION: 1993
FEAST DAY: 12 APRIL
PATRONAGE: YOUNG PEOPLE, THE SICK
ATTRIBUTES: DISCALCED CARMELITE HABIT, CRUCIFIX

Theresa was a nun who became the first saint born in Chile. She was named Juana Enriqueta Josephina de Los Sagrados Corazones Fernandez Solar at birth, but her name was changed after entering the convent of Discalced Carmelites in the city of Los Andes – she had been inspired by St Therese of Lisieux after reading her life story. However, within a year, Theresa had fallen ill, and she died at the age of 19. Theresa is said to have been vain, headstrong and quick to anger when she was younger and is much admired for losing these characteristics and dedicating herself to God.

ST FAUSTINA KOWALSKA (1905–1938)

PLACE OF BIRTH: GŁOGOWIEC, POLAND

DATE OF CANONIZATION: 2000

FEAST DAY: 5 OCTOBER

PATRONAGE: MERCY

ATTRIBUTES: DIVINE MERCY IMAGE

Faustina had apparitions of Jesus that inspired devotion to the Divine Mercy, an image of Jesus that Faustina described as 'God's loving mercy'. She joined a convent in the Polish capital Warsaw at the age of 20, and with the help of Father Michael Sopocko commissioned an artist to paint the first Divine Mercy image based on her vision of Jesus. Eugene Kazimierowski's image became the object of wide devotion, especially as, before her death in 1938, Faustina had predicted there would be 'a terrible, terrible war'. By 1941, the devotion had reached the United States, and millions of copies of Divine Mercy prayer cards were printed and distributed worldwide.

MOTHER TERESA OF CALCUTTA (1910–1997)

PLACE OF BIRTH: SKOPJE, NORTH MACEDONIA

DATE OF CANONIZATION: 2016

FEAST DAY: 5 SEPTEMBER

PATRONAGE: MISSIONARIES OF CHARITY

ATTRIBUTES: WHITE SARI WITH BLUE TRIM

Of Kosovo Albanian descent, Mother Teresa was born Anjeze Gonxhe Bojaxhiu in Skopje, North Macedonia, which at the time was part of the Ottoman Empire. At the age of 18, she joined the Sisters of Loreto in Rathfarnham, Ireland, to learn English and become a missionary. In India, she chose to be named after St Therese of Lisieux. For years, she was a teacher there before being called to tend to the poor. She founded the Missionaries of Charity, which expanded rapidly. Mother Teresa became a globally recognized figure, winning the Nobel Peace Prize, brokering a ceasefire between Israelis and Palestinians, and caring for famine victims in Ethiopia and radiation victims near Chernobyl. By 2012, her institute had more than 4500 nuns across 133 countries.

OSCAR ROMERO (1917–1980)

PLACE OF BIRTH: CIUDAD BARRIOS, EL SALVADOR
DATE OF CANONIZATION: 2018
FEAST DAY: 24 MARCH
PATRONAGE: EL SALVADOR, THE AMERICAS
ATTRIBUTES: CROWN OF MARTYRDOM, MARTYR'S PALM

Oscar Romero was archbishop of San Salvador when he was shot by an assassin while celebrating mass. The Truth Commission for El Salvador concluded that Major Roberto D'Aubuisson, a death squad leader and later founder of the Nationalist Republican Alliance, had ordered the killing. Romero had spoken out against social injustice and the escalating conflict between El Salvador's military government and left-wing insurgents. Pope Francis said that Oscar Romero's 'ministry was distinguished by his particular attention to the most poor and marginalized'.

ST JOHN PAUL II (1920–2005)

PLACE OF BIRTH: WADOWICE, POLAND

DATE OF CANONIZATION: 2014

FEAST DAY: 22 OCTOBER

PATRONAGE: POLAND, ARCHDIOCESE OF KRAKÓW

ATTRIBUTES: PAPAL VESTMENTS

John Paul II was pope from 1978 to his death in 2005, and as such, he was also bishop of Rome and sovereign of the Vatican City State. Born Krol Jozef Wojtyla in Poland, under Nazi occupation he worked in harsh conditions in a quarry, barely surviving after being hit by an army truck and a tram. He then studied theology and became a priest, rising to be archbishop of Krakow. He took the name John Paul as pope, in honour of the man who preceded him, John Paul I, who died 33 days into the role. John Paul was the only non-Italian pope since Adrian VI in the 16th century and the third longest-serving pope (after Pius IX in the 19th century and St Peter). One of the most travelled world leaders in history – often in his 'popemobile' vehicle – John Paul himself canonized 483 people.

Picture credits